THE
POWER
OF
ACCEPTANCE

ANNEMARIE POSTMA

THE
POWER
OF
ACCEPTANCE

A GUIDE TO ENDING THE
SEARCH FOR PERFECTION BY
SURRENDERING TO WHAT IS

WATKINS PUBLISHING

LONDON

What if, starting today, we stop thinking in terms of what's lacking and imperfect?

What if we no longer think everything needs to be fixed, healed or improved?

What if we stop trying to change reality with the power of our thoughts and intentions?

What if we start to believe that the Universe does not make mistakes?

This edition first published in the UK and USA 2013 by
Watkins Publishing Limited, Sixth Floor,
75 Wells Street, London W1T 3QH

A member of Osprey Group

Osprey Publishing
PO Box 3985
New York, NY 10185-3985

1 3 5 7 9 10 8 6 4 2

Designed by Gail Jones

Printed and bound by CPI Group (UK) Ltd, Croydon, CR0 4YY

ISBN: 978-1-78028-760-7

www.watkinspublishing.co.uk

contents

Foreword 9

Introduction 15

1 Happiness for Experts 25

2 How Does the Search Begin? 31

3 The Unique Balance Between Intention and Surrender:
A Conversation with Dr Joe Dispenza 37

4 Living in the Wisdom of Uncertainty 47

5 Embracing the Mystery 59

6 Becoming Your Own Answer 69

7 Consciousness Over Matter 77

8 How We Create Reality 87

9 A Dialogue with Life: A Conversation with Gregg Braden 95

10 Stop Working on Yourself 111

11 What You Resist Persists 121

12 Reconnecting with the Cosmic Frequencies: A Conversation
with Dr Eric Pearl 129

13 The Tragedy of the Endless Search 141

14 Life is Not a Fight that Needs to be Won: A Conversation
with Lynne McTaggart 151

15 Balance Between 'Doing' and 'Being' 163

16 Constructing Your Inner Infrastructure: A Conversation
with Prof William Tiller 173

In Closing 185

Special Thanks 191

Bibliography 192

foreword

Life is so much easier when you don't resist it.
Reality already is the best thing that could be manifested.
When you realize this, you're home-free.

– BYRON KATIE

To embrace reality is an act of total renewal. When we dare to see things as they truly are, it immediately brings us a feeling of liberation, strength and healing. Therefore, it is no coincidence that Buddhists describe 'experiencing God' as being 'completely present' in reality. However, in order to 'land' yourself fully in reality, you need to surrender to it first. To surrender means to let go of the control you think you have in your life. It means releasing your preconceived thoughts and notions about how you think your life should be. It is all about no longer forcing your personal will onto reality. In fact, to surrender is a celebration of real freedom.

*

Life is so much easier when you don't resist it,
when you stop hitting the brakes.

*

I'll admit, surrender is a big word. But the meaning of it is actually quite basic.

To surrender means that you give your full and undivided attention to a situation. Most of the time these are very common situations. Instead of being upset about your computer that crashed, the train you just missed or the friend who is not reacting the way you had hoped or expected, you can also choose and decide to simply accept these things. To surrender also means taking the 'I' out of a thing and/or situations. Without realizing it, we are constantly hitting the brakes on our lives.

Why? Because our 'I' always has an opinion about everything and is filled with illusions and incorrect assumptions. Rarely has anything in my life gone the way I had hoped, expected or thought. Those were some heavy blows for my 'I'. However, in hindsight, I can see that everything turned out just fine. During those moments when the 'I' receives some bumps and bruises along the way and slows down, that is exactly when space is created to truly *be*.

Life is so much easier when you don't resist it and stop hitting the brakes. By offering so much resistance against reality, you tend to miss the full experience happening right now and, therefore, you're missing the true beauty of life. I am increasingly surprised that we have such a difficult time understanding something which is, in fact, so natural; or rather how bad we are at applying it to our everyday lives. Or as the great Dutch sinologist and Taoist, Kristofer Schipper once said: 'The fight against the natural course of things is perhaps the greatest evil of our time.'

*

What is good for you is usually whatever is happening right now.

*

I have written about acceptance in many of my other books. However, this time I would like to go deeper into the subject. We can look at how and why those moments when you put the brakes on your life occur. Instead of denying the truth about yourself and your life, or reducing or rejecting it, we're going to take a look at it in a relaxed manner and without any judgement.

Our life is communicating with us. Just like our body, not only does it show us something about ourselves (because it's a reflection of our consciousness at the moment), but it also speaks to us. It tells us which areas within ourselves deserve and need attention, what limiting thoughts and convictions we are unnecessarily holding on to, what our deepest fears are, how faithful and truthful we are to ourselves and which parts of us need love. So, when you think that everything is going 'wrong' in your life at the moment, realize that that is nothing more than an illusion that your mind has created.

In reality, you are functioning exactly as you should be and in precisely the right circumstances. You have exactly the right relationship, perfect health and the perfect weight, even when your 'I' doesn't seem to agree. You probably think everything should be different and that only you know what is really good for you. But whatever is good for you is usually exactly what is happening, right here and right now. What your life looks like, and how you are right now, is exactly what is needed to further your spiritual growth, to complete the inner homework you've been given.

*

*The fight against the natural course of things
is perhaps the greatest evil of our time.*

*

At this point you're probably thinking, 'Yeah right, whatever you say! There are so many things wrong with my life. Not to mention the people that are seriously ill. And what about welfare mothers with four children? Do they have to simply 'accept' their situation, too?'

No, you don't have to do anything. When it comes down to it, our personality consciousness has a free will. So, the questions are: do you embrace life as it is – or do you fight it? Do you accept life's challenges – or do you resist them? Our earthly life is a stage where we can act out all of the scenarios our soul chose for us before we were born – or we can ignore them. What kind of attitude we choose to take on towards our experiences is entirely up to us. In this respect, right or wrong doesn't exist. Our soul doesn't think in time and it is always aware of its immortality. It only wants to grow. It has no attachment to the amount of time that is needed for that.

*

If you dare to ask yourself certain questions in all honesty, usually the answer is nearby.

*

Imagine everything that happens in life happens for a reason. What would that mean? What do the challenges you meet along the way tell you about what you are here to learn, what have you come to teach others and what do you have to give to this life?

By asking yourself these questions, the challenges in your life will suddenly have a different meaning and significance. When you choose to approach things in this manner, you will find yourself going down a completely new road. A road which offers a more loving space to everything that happens in our lives. Do you need to be a New Age guru or believe in hocus-pocus in order to do this? Not at all, don't worry! This is really a book for everyone. For anyone who is curious and eager to learn – anyone who is interested in real personal growth.

ANNEMARIE

introduction

Learning to want what is
Some things ... arrive in their own mysterious hour,
on their own terms and not yours,
to be seized or relinquished forever.

– GAIL GODWIN

I think acceptance is the most beautiful word there is. Buddhists have an even more beautiful term for it with an even deeper meaning:

Tathata
Tathata means unconditionally saying 'yes'. It means saying 'yes' so deeply and completely that there is no longer any division within yourself, absolutely no denial within yourself, and 'no' no longer exists within you. You become completely one with your 'yes'. The moment you say 'yes' unconditionally to life as it is right now, you step into the complete sum of wisdom and endless possibilities. The moment you can say 'yes' to yourself, exactly as you are right now, you instantly create space for real development, and you create wholeness and healing within yourself and in your existence.

Dukkha

Because of my theosophical background, I've been studying the differences between Buddhist and Western thinking since my early adolescence. One of the big differences between our way of thinking and Buddhist thinking is that we are incredibly conditioned. When things become difficult in our life, when they don't come easily or go smoothly, we think something has gone 'wrong'. When things don't go as we planned, thought or dreamed, we think life is going in the wrong direction and that things will not end well with us. So instead of saying 'yes' to life, we quietly start to say 'no', and without even realizing it, we hit the brakes on our life. We are really focused on controlling and dividing everything into categories: good or bad. For Buddhists, everything is just as it is. When things don't go smoothly and there is conflict, the Buddhists call this dukkha. This translates into something like 'life is suffering'. Only they don't give the word 'suffer' the same loaded meaning as we Westerners do.

*

If we suffer, it is because we try to change life as it is into life as we want it.

*

According to Buddha, if we suffer, it is only because we are constantly trying to change life as it is into life as we want it to be. We want to shape the reality of this moment, or the experience before us, into how we think it should be. We bring this struggle upon ourselves constantly. Which causes those of us who live in the West to always have the feeling of dukkha; that something is always wrong. We feel that this very moment is not quite how it could or should have been.

Giving up resistance

There are countless examples of people (and I've experienced this personally so many times as well) who show us that the moment we take our foot off the break, loosen the reins on our will and our wishes and decide to give up our resistance to what is, that the feeling of dukkha disappears and a sense of great ease returns to our life. Often, seemingly inexplicable things then happen. Resistance disappears. Things you've wanted to happen for a long time suddenly happen. You find yourself increasingly experiencing moments of 'synchronicity' (meaningful coincidences) and start to feel better in your own skin and more at home in your own life. When you can say to yourself, 'Pain and suffering are part of life and I am not afraid to experience what is', then your whole relationship with pain and suffering will change. You may not see an immediate change in your direct surroundings, but you will begin to see life differently, and it will also feel different, because you are no longer ruled by suffering.

There's a huge miracle hidden in the calm acceptance of all that is. If there is one thing I have learned over the past few years, it is that changes happen the moment you think nothing needs to be changed anymore. This may sound like one of those hollow spiritual phrases – it certainly would sound like that to you if you are still having difficulty in finding acceptance – but it really isn't. To truly become the master of your own life does not mean you can force it into what you want it to be with the snap of a finger. No, the real road to mastering your life begins with facing what is real and true. The key to inner peace, happiness, health and success is not found in learning to change what is, but in actually learning to want what is. You always think you know what's good for you, but, in fact, what is good for us is often precisely whatever is happening right now.

But how do you do it? How do you accept your life as it is when, at this very moment, it doesn't look or feel anything like how you want it to be? How do you accept yourself when you're not even comfortable in your own skin and have constant inferior thoughts about yourself? Well, this is precisely what this book is about!

*

How do you accept yourself
when you're not even comfortable in your own skin?

*

There is no magic pill you can take to find instant self-acceptance and acceptance of life in general with all of its trials and tribulations. If that were the case, there wouldn't be so many dissatisfied people in the world constantly fighting against their reality. Accepting life as it is and accepting your body, for example, just as it is, can seem like an almost impossible task. Don't be discouraged if you don't succeed right away in creating space for reality, or if you find it threatening or frightening at times. Of course it feels this way; it would be strange if it didn't. You are venturing out into new and unknown territory. To give up your resistance also means letting go of your familiar patterns. We all know that for most people breaking patterns is one of the most difficult things to do.

Practise progress, not perfection
Don't punish and judge yourself either. Remember: it's a process, a journey, a road of trial and error. I once read, 'Practise progress, not perfection'. Good advice. This works just like a growth or development that we experience: two steps forward, one step back. That's how it goes. Not only for you, but for everyone. Take a look around you: most people would prefer to go to the other end of the world to visit a guru or a fancy retreat instead of accepting life as it is in the here and now.

*

Acceptance is the road to enlightenment.

*

Acceptance sounds like something simple: you just relax, kick back and accept. Well, it's not that simple! It has nothing to do with passively letting everything happen. Learning how to do this is the core of everything, the true power of creation that drives everything, the secret to everything. You will gradually start to feel and understand the reasons why as you read on.

We will also clear up misconceptions, such as acceptance meaning you are lazy, passive or fatalistic. And rest assured, we will also answer questions such as: What about 'personal sustainability'? Isn't it true that we can mould and shape our own lives into what we want them to be with the power of thought and intention? Another question is: How do acceptance and personal sustainability compare? Are they opposites or not?

I discussed all of these issues with well-known international, spiritual bestselling authors and new scientists, from Lynne McTaggart, Gregg Braden and Eric Pearl, to Joe Dispenza and my favourite professor, William Tiller (from the famous scientific documentary *What the Bleep Do We Know!?*). I had the privilege of meeting them all personally, and I spoke with them about the healing power of acceptance, and whether that power – just like the power of intention – can be measured. But the central question I asked them was:

'What if, starting today, we stop thinking in terms of what's lacking and imperfect? What if we even let go of the concept of the power of our thoughts and intention? What if we no longer think things need to be fixed, healed or improved? What kind of power and energy is released when we function in full acceptance and put to rest our eternal search for enlightenment and freedom?'

I believe (and experience this every day) that if we let go of our fixation on the personal sustainability of our existence and replace the question 'What do I want in life?' with the question 'What does life want from me?', then the greatest power in the universe is released – infinitely more powerful and stronger than anything we can manifest with our conscience through intention and thought. It is a power that is greatly underestimated and ignored because we are so unbelievably afraid of losing control.

I am even convinced that this same power can be measured. I believe you can measure what complete and deep relaxing acceptance does to someone's body, health and vibrational field (and therefore the effect on his or her surroundings). I spoke about this to the amazing and progressive scientist Konstantin Korotkov. He participated in the Intention Experiment with Lynne McTaggart.

*

As soon as we can look at life without inner resistance,
it will be the beginning of living life from a new
and magical perspective.

*

You will find some of these conversations in this book. They were long conversations, sometimes hours long. You will not find them in their entirety here, but I will share the core of what they said about acceptance. Many of the people I spoke with had to really take their time and think about these questions before giving their answer. This didn't surprise me. Because they are, after all, each in their own individual way, focused on the concept of personal sustainability, using the power of thoughts and intention to influence the world outside of us.

"Yes, but," I asked them, "what if, in the meantime, this has become passé? What if there is more to it than that? Something that could help improve the quality of our lives in a radical new way, without causing radical changes to the outside structure of our lives? Without negotiating? Without doing anything, but only saying yes to everything that happens in reality?"

*

Each moment we open our heart to reality
reveals the underlying perfection of our earthly existence.

*

I hope you will enjoy this book, and that you will join me in this acceptance experiment. What would your life be like if you allowed yourself to abandon all of your ideas about how your life should look and how you could be? How would your life feel if you no longer had a judgement about everything that takes place in reality? How would you feel if you allowed yourself to be a whole human being? How would you live your life if you no longer feared your feelings? How and who would you love?

Let go of your expectations, including the ones about yourself, and allow yourself to melt into the natural rhythm of everything and everyone around you. Quietly experience what it is like, for you, your health, your life and your environment, when you cease the constant discussion and negotiations with that which is. Feel what happens when you criticize reality, and also feel what happens when you stop meddling and interfering in your life and leave it up to life to decide what should or should not happen.

*

Creating something with sheer will power
means forcing something to happen by manipulating reality.

*

The era we live in now invites us to find the truth, to live in truth, to focus on our self and to shape the things around us only from our inner truth. It's important that you do things in your own way and at the right moment for you; that your actions or inactions and your motives are clear and pure. Impurity does not work anymore; any non-truths – in the broadest sense – are quickly brought to light now. We live in a time of purging, deep cleansing and learning to relax – within ourselves and into the world around us.

It is about diving deep into the depths of yourself, in everything you do or don't do, to find the silence that resides at your core and to speak from that core, or decide not to speak from it, to take action or not to take action.

Every Eastern belief system shows us the same thing: before you start moving, connect first to your centre of silence, your inertia and your power. It is important to take your time with this, because anything that is not properly anchored in your core will quickly fall apart and disappear. Make sure you stay truthfully with yourself and with the real core of things. The right moment that will put you in motion and action will come in its own time.

Living according to Sacred Instructions

What can go wrong when you stay faithful to what you feel and to what is true? What can go wrong if you listen to your inner voice and feel what life wants from you? The answer is: absolutely nothing. The funny thing is that we arrogantly think we are always in control. But there is also something called 'the soul's agenda' and a higher order of all things. We only make bad decisions when we are no longer in touch with our soul and this higher order. You see that in the end it's not about what we want, but starting to listen to what life wants from us, and stop pushing and breaking through these Sacred Instructions with our own will power.

Sensing momentum and anticipating on it – that is creation. When you feel at your core: yes, that is the time to come into action or consciously decide not to. In 2007, I wrote the predecessor to this book, *The Deeper Secret*. One particular morning I just knew: now is the time for the sequel. I didn't come up with this in my own mind, nor was it part of some well thought-out marketing strategy. It just came to me.

*

Sensing momentum and anticipating it – that is creation.

*

For many of my readers – maybe you are a coach or therapist – this can be a new approach to helping guide others towards gaining more inner freedom. My own experience has convinced me that the moment we can look at life without any inner resistance is the beginning of living life from a new and magical perspective. Each moment we truly open our hearts to the experience before us will reveal the underlying perfection of our earthly existence.

happiness
for experts

When you realize there is nothing lacking,
the whole world belongs to you.

– LAO TSE

Happiness is something for later

Recently, my husband Robin and I attended a theatre show by one of my favourite Dutch comedians, Lenette van Dongen. The stage design was simple yet impressive, and consisted of a high mountain with a waterfall; she entered the stage climbing the mountain. Of course, the mountain symbolized our personal uphill climb through life, the ups and the downs, but also our hopes of one day reaching that one unknown destination, the place where the big reward awaits you – the reward you will receive for all that amazing (inner) work you have done with so much effort and dedication. The place where you think: OK, I have finally arrived; now I know the true meaning of life and what it's all about.

But soon the character finds herself stuck in a general feeling of powerlessness. She comes to the conclusion that it's actually not all that interesting to continually focus on the meaning of things, but that it is far more important to live your life to the fullest extent right now, with an open heart. In doing so, you give it true meaning.

To be grateful and happy in life but not so that everything goes your way. This Lenette refers to as 'happiness for beginners'. To be capable of overcoming the difficult periods in life, to change something negative into something positive and to recognize the lessons hidden in these experiences and to take action. This she calls 'happiness for the advanced'. However, to be sincerely grateful and happy, even when you find yourself in the middle of one of life's biggest storms, you still don't want it to be different or to change it. This is the kind of happiness where nothing has to be done or is required, where nothing needs to be achieved and success is not demanded. Happiness is where all the thinking, searching, striving, musts and wants are taken out. This she calls 'happiness for experts'.

Happiness for experts, now that's a keeper! Yes, because learning to accept life is easy as long as everything goes the way you planned or thought it should. But when things don't go the way we planned, something else is being asked of us. Something that goes beyond reactions like: They won't get me down! I'm a survivor! I'll show them, or I'll prove to them just exactly how spiritual I am by how I will handle this!

*

The greatest changes occur when we surrender our constant urge to control.

*

What emerges, for any sensitive listener, so beautifully from Lenette's show, is that your life becomes far more relaxed once you surrender the urge to always want to understand and control everything. The greatest changes often occur when you stop wanting things to be different and then they are. One of the biggest downfalls of the 'spiritual path' is that it continually tells you that you aren't there yet. By all means, you must first travel down some long path and climb a giant mountain. When you reach the top and do everything just right, you may find your unconditional birthright and all the answers you seek. Not now, no, but always later. Happiness is something for later. Happiness is something you have to earn and work hard for. So it's no surprise you still have a long way to go. Something needs to be achieved, something is definitely lacking. After all, you still haven't reached the top of that mountain yet, that place where everything is good, clear and safe.

In her show, Lenette van Dongen puts this theory to rest, without using a lot of words or complicated scenarios. At the end of the show, after a lot of climbing, struggling and sweating, she finally reaches the top of the mountain. Satisfied, she takes a break and looks around. She did it! She didn't give up, life won't get the best of her, and she persisted, came, saw and conquered. She had arrived. Mission accomplished: at peace with the 'now'. With a satisfied and almost smug smile, she sat there taking it all in.

*

The so-called path of working on yourself is often nothing more than a long detour to the now.

*

Suddenly she noticed an old lady was up there with her at the top of the same mountain. How could this be? Turns out that during her search, struggle and focus on what she would find up there, she completely missed the fact that on the other side of the mountain there was an elevator. That was so unfair! How could this lady, without professional help or mountain-climbing gear, with her support hose, get up there so easily, while Lenette had struggled so hard to get to the top?

The moral of the story: the so-called path of working on yourself is often nothing more than a long detour to the now. The real spiritual road is not one that leads somewhere but one that allows you to be fully present in the moment and allows you to reflect on who you are from the deepest part of your being.

Summary

1} The greatest changes occur when we no longer believe things need to be different.

2} Real transformation takes place when we surrender the constant urge to control and understand everything.

3} The biggest downfall of the spiritual path is that it tells you that you aren't there yet. First, you must travel down a path and climb a giant mountain. Where, at the top, and only if you do everything just right, you may find your unconditional birthright and the answers you seek.

4} The so-called path of working on yourself is often nothing more than a long detour to the now.

5} The real spiritual road is not a road that leads somewhere but one that allows you to be fully present in the moment now and allows you to reflect on who you are from the deepest part of your being.

how does the search begin?

As long as there's seeking, there isn't understanding.

– WAYNE LIQUORMAN

Is it possible to feel great in a life full of problems? Newsflash: you have no other choice. Well, OK, that's not entirely true. To be more specific, you have two choices: 1. Be unhappy in a life full of problems; 2. Be happy in a life full of problems. Because if there is one thing you know for sure in this earthly life, it is that problems will always arise. Life will always be full of contradictions and challenges, and we are on an impossible mission if we deny or avoid that fact. Yet, most of the time that is exactly what we do: whether you have a problem in your relationship, with your children, your parents or your health, a conflict at work, or you have no idea what your mission, purpose or goal is in life. The core of the endless search for spiritual enlightenment is always resistance.

In essence it is always an unwillingness to offer space to that which happens in reality in the moment and to fully experience it. You would much rather believe the experience isn't real, or trade it in for something else, for something you would prefer. That way, reality as it presents itself is always wrong in any case. There's something not quite right about it, something is lacking, or there is actually something you presume shouldn't be there.

*

Life doesn't ask us for our opinion,
I'm sure you've discovered this by now?

*

To think we should banish our problems is like banishing life itself. Dutch author Kristofer Schipper says it beautifully:

"At the deepest core of life is a primal type of chaos. Somehow we always desire to return to it and yet, at the same time, we long for absolute security and immortality. But ultimately our lives are governed by chaos. Nothing is ever certain. The non-duality (and therefore the peace) returns only when you let go of your resistance, when you no longer create dividing lines between happiness and unhappiness and take on the following attitude towards everything: everything is welcome in my world."

*

Our lives are governed by chaos. Nothing is ever certain.

*

We aren't used to looking at things or thinking in this way. We're all little gossip columnists and movie critics who think that life is sitting around and waiting for our opinion. Most of us have the inner belief: everything is welcome in my life – but only on my conditions. However, life doesn't ask for our opinion or judgement – surely you've discovered this by now? To allow this truth into our consciousness sounds easier than it is. Just look at how easily we lose our minds when we don't feel good, are stuck or struggling with the patterns we cannot seem to break. "Nope, this is not happening. That's not allowed. We have to do something about that as soon as possible, because it indicates 'failure'." You are always left feeling that you must be doing something wrong. Otherwise, you would be happy, right?

*

We're all little gossip columnists and movie critics
who think that life is sitting around waiting for our opinion.

*

So we go into therapy or we trade in our guru for a mental coach, and so on, bury ourselves in yoga, meditation, mindfulness, NLP, regression therapy and silence retreats, or we take a much needed sabbatical. Anything is better than the here and now. Everything and everywhere else is more important and better than right here, right now. Working on ourselves – that's what it's all about. Everyone is constantly busy to make sure they feel good, are happy, healthy and in balance. But in the end, it doesn't seem to be making any of us very happy or left feeling very energetic. To feel good and to be in balance constantly is quite an effort and often leads to feelings of discomfort and inadequacy. It is the eternal search for the better version of yourself.

How does this search begin? Well, think about it: usually with the idea that you are not good enough as you are right now, your life is incomplete as it is right now. You feel uncomfortable in your own skin and in your own current reality, so something must be done: you have to get to a higher consciousness, you have to feel more whole, you have to remember who you were in your previous life, you have to know your mission in life, you have to know why you are the way you are, you need to become more peaceful and still, you need to be healthier, break your patterns, be at peace with old traumas, balance out your karma and get rid of that ego. That pretty much sums up the fallacies on which the eternal search is based. Before you know it, you find yourself at home on your couch, completely exhausted, because you have no idea where to even begin, or you are feverishly shopping in the new consciousness industry, searching for a better version of yourself.

*

As long as we are searching, we are by definition
not present in the now.

*

The search has become a kind of 'must' for both the material and immaterial human being. Some interesting studies were done (including one by *The Economist* in 2007) which show that people with an increase in prosperity or financial gain do not, by definition, become happier. Yet we all continue to strive for that prosperity, status, power and sex, because we think it will bring us happiness and fulfilment. Those who live consciously are also painfully aware of the fact that he or she is a constant work in progress, meaning they are still not 'there' yet.

These are spiritual concepts and definitions that we must get rid of as fast as possible. Because as long as we are searching for something more, better, different or more complete, we are not present in the now and therefore not in contact with our creative core.

"Let yourself be fed by all things, so your heart can roam freely," said Taoist poet and philosopher Zhuang Zi. "Always place yourself in the inevitable in order to feed the centre. Then you have achieved the highest possible. Why would you do something only so you can get something in return, instead of simply fulfilling your task? That's where the whole problem lies!"

Summary

1} The core of your endless search for spiritual enlightenment is always resistance. In essence it is always an unwillingness to offer space to that which happens in reality in the moment and to fully experience it. You would much rather believe the experience isn't real or trade it in for something else.

2} The search always begins with the idea that you are not good enough as you are now, your life is incomplete as it is right now.

3} As long as we continue to search for something more, better, different or complete, then we are, by definition, not present in the now, and we cannot get into contact with our creative core. First of all: there is nothing else but now. Secondly: you are here. You are already in the now. So what do you think you will find outside of the now?

the unique balance between intention and surrender

A CONVERSATION WITH DR JOE DISPENZA

Live your life as if your prayers have already been answered.
That is surrender.

– DR JOE DISPENZA

Balance between intention and surrender

Just how does the power of acceptance work? I spoke about this with, among others, neuroscientist Dr Joe Dispenza. If you have ever seen the award-winning documentary *What the Bleep Do*

We Know!? and its sequel *What the Bleep!? – Down the Rabbit Hole*, then you will know exactly who I mean. In the film he tells us, for instance, how you can consciously create your own day.

About 20 years ago, Dispenza was hit by a car and ended up in hospital with multiple fractures in his spine. His doctors told him he was facing a lifetime of pain and physical discomfort, but he refused to believe them and literally 'thought' himself better. Three months later, against all odds, he was just as mobile as ever before.

*

There is a unique balance between intention and surrender.

*

Joe Dispenza has devoted many years to the study of the human spirit – how it works, how we store information, why we repeat the same patterns over and over and how we can create our daily reality with our thinking. In his book *The Science of Changing Your Mind* and also in his documentary *Your Immortal Brain*, Dr Joe Dispenza explains to us how our brain develops and learns new things and how we can gain control over our thoughts. But does gaining control over our thoughts automatically mean gaining control over our lives?

Can we force our will onto the physical world with the power of our thoughts and intentions? Dispenza's opinion on this offers a prominent place in regard to the power of acceptance, surrender and gratefulness.

"There is a unique balance between intention and surrender. Intention is intended to help you clear up what you want and how you see the future before you. That future vision has potentially been around in the 'quantum model' for a very long time, because all potential possibilities exist side by side in the quantum field."

Clarifying exactly what you want is therefore a conscious action in order to be part of that potential in the quantum field.

It is the absolute first step in creation. Intention itself does not create reality; it is just one of the creative elements that sets it in motion.

*

Intention itself does not create reality.

*

Dispenza sees surrender as a crucial part of the creation process. "If you really surrender, then you also trust completely. And if you really trust yourself, then you understand that there is a field of consciousness (a quantum field of consciousness) that responds to who you are. Not only to what you think. No, to your whole vibration, your whole consciousness. That intelligence listens to you very carefully. It creates things that match exactly how you think and feel. To surrender to that intelligence means that right now, without any change in your physical world, you can get to a higher state of consciousness, a state of gratitude. It means that you experience a shift in energy and elevate yourself to the feeling that you are and will be totally taken care of, the realization that there is something bigger than you handling all the details.

"This is obviously something our analytical mind finds difficult to understand because it thinks: how can I connect to a feeling that belongs to an experience which hasn't even taken place in reality yet?" With a great unadulterated, nasal, American monotone, Dispenza says: "That's Newtonian physics." What he means by this is that it is the world of cause and effect. Something changes in the outside world, we react to it, and only then does something change inside of us. The quantum model sees this precisely the other way around: it causes an effect. Instead of being a product of it, the consciousness is the creator of the physical world. This means that you first have to surrender to the greater power in order to make contact with it. You have to fall in love with how you will feel later, before you even have any proof that any of it will take place. That is surrender: to live life in a way as if all your prayers have already been answered.

Letting go so you can receive

"Maybe you think to yourself: what a bunch of nonsense, it's not possible. But that is the quantum model," says Dispenza.

"First you have to come from a place of total trust with yourself before what you have in mind can take place. That means that you are connected to the outcome of your wish, but have no desire to influence or control the outcome. This is something very important when it comes to creation, but also very difficult to understand for people who really want to change something in their lives. You have to completely and unconditionally let go of what you desire the most before you can receive it."

*

You first have to surrender to the greater power in order to make contact with it.

*

"The essence of the quantum model is that the outcome is always unpredictable. The Newtonian model, however, is extremely predictable. And when something is reasonably predictable, then our analytical mind starts to interfere, the ego wants to dominate and control the creation process, and influence the outcome. That's exactly where we are in the way of the creation process. It's the moment where we block the higher intelligence, stopping the flow."

I thought Dispenza's explanation was really clear and to the point. No, we don't create only with our thinking but with our whole (conscious) being. The more we trust and, therefore, the more relaxation enters our vibration frequency, and the more receptive we become. Then it becomes easier for the things that we need to come to us. The heavy load, the pressure and necessity to get something done are no longer there. When the necessity is gone, there is freedom and miracles can happen. I experience this in my own life every day.

The quantum creation clue

This is the real quantum creation clue. It means that, when we send a specified shopping list and *The Secret*-type of demands into the universe, we are frantically trying to gain and keep control of our lives. We've got something in mind, we visualize what our life should look like (and what we need to achieve it) and we place our order as if the Universe were a roadside diner. But where there is a need for control, there is no freedom, and where there is no freedom, things cannot flow freely.

It's very Western of us to think that everything is in our own control. But hidden below the surface of this need to control is usually fear, insecurity or a lack of confidence in ourselves, life and in the higher order of things, which we try to banish this way. Understandable? Yes, of course. When I say that the basis of creation is a complete desire-less inner peace, don't think: Oh, that's easily done. Living one full day in total peace is already a huge accomplishment.

Survival mode blocks creation

Why do we find acceptance so difficult? How can we bring ourselves in the right state of consciousness to help us accept reality? Dispenza asks me: "Who has difficulty with acceptance? The mind only wants to remain in control when it lives in survival mode. When you live in that mode, you believe the outside world is more real than your inner world. This mode also sees to it that your reaction to things engages your primal nervous system, which creates chemical reactions using emotions like anger, fear and aggression. This is not just some 'metaphysical nonsense' but actual biology. Once this chemical reaction is triggered, the person becomes egotistical. They become a person who will always try to manage and control everything, who wants to know where he stands in order to feel safe."

*

Giving up control is the prerequisite
to being able to create.

*

"Survival and creation do not go together, they are each other's opposite," says Dispenza. "It's impossible to be in control and be in a state of creation at the same time; giving up control is the prerequisite to being able to create. When you create, you are completely selfless. The moment that you become selfless there is a biological reaction; a shift takes place and the chemistry of your brain changes the way the brain works. True creation takes place when you forget your you. Acceptance is the road from selfishness to selflessness."

Dispenza calls this the 'biology of change'. He says: "For most people, change is so difficult because the survival emotions are very addictive and they cloud your perception. So when someone is unemployed, has no money in the bank and you speak to them about surrender, letting go and acceptance, they cannot even hear you. Why not? Because their survival mode overrules their perception, it disrupts their ability for acceptance."

*

Acceptance is the road from selfishness to selflessness.

*

"These survival emotions are a kind of 'layer' or 'mask', and those layers block the intelligence which has given you life, that allows your heart to beat, that digests your food – in short, the spiritual aspect that rules and keeps your body together. When we start to peel away those layers, remove the masks and begin to change, the higher intelligence can stream through and from us again. From that moment on we become happier, more loving, thoughtful, creative and generous. That is actually our natural state of being. So feeling good can only exist in the absence of emotional addictions," Dispenza says. "When you have freed yourself of your inner limitations, it automatically has a psychological effect: the heart cannot help but to open itself up, because it is the place where all the energy is flowing to. The side effect of breaking the survival patterns and that type of transformation is that the intelligent energy that flows through you is very cohesive and pulsating, orderly, systematic and balanced. This is what we experience as joy and happiness."

Conditional living

Most of the time we don't even know that we are functioning in survival mode; we've started to feel this as a natural state of being. Often, we are not really aware of how we are sitting around, hoping and waiting for different circumstances to arrive so we can relax and be present in reality at some point in the future. The majority of people are living conditional and permanently postponed lives: first the new house, solve the money problems, recover from the illness or my mother or father needs to get better, first I want to learn to accept life and myself. Only then can I be present and relaxed.

We constantly attach conditions on being ourselves. It is as if you have to earn life, which causes us to have a thousand reasons to postpone truly living our lives. The sad part is that while you think you're doing something positive by doing this, you are, in fact, minimizing the possibilities of creating a new reality (the one you really want for yourself). In hoping for a better situation, you are in such a narrow state of consciousness that you are no longer aligned to the greater whole. You cannot see outside of it. When that connection is gone, you can no longer receive the message, and there is no possible exchange between you and the universe.

*

When you live in total trust, there is no need to visualize.

*

It's important to remain part of the whole, so it allows you to be free and open. That way, communication can take place between your consciousness and the all-consciousness: what fits and belongs to you, because your future in life can never be a goal, because it is always a result of something. It's the result of becoming who you can be in this life, to do what's needed to get there and take responsibility, being honest to yourself about yourself and courageously face your fears and travel your own inner road. It's also the result of living your life in total trust. When you live in total trust, there is no need to visualize. You are already in tune with what will help you to do well in life.

*

*Getting what you want is the result of going
beyond your neediness.*

*

It is a cosmic law that says – no matter how paradoxical it sounds – that when there is something you really want or need, life always gives it to you on one condition: that you have transcended the neediness and feel free inside. What you get then is so much more than you could have ever hoped for, wished or visualized.

Summary

1} Intention is meant to help you clarify what you want and how you see your future.

2} That future vision has potentially been around in the quantum model for a very long time, because all potential possibilities exist side by side in the quantum field.

3} To clarify exactly what you want is therefore a conscious action in order to be part of that potential in the quantum field.

4} To surrender is crucial in the creation process. Surrender means living your life as if all your prayers have already been answered.

5} First you have to come from a place of total trust with yourself before what you have in mind can take place.

6} That means that you are connected to the outcome of your wish, but have no desire to influence or control the outcome.

7} It is a cosmic law that says when there is something you really want or need, life always gives it to you on one condition: that you have transcended the neediness and feel free inside.

living in
the wisdom
of uncertainty

Always we hope someone else has the answer,
some other place will be better,
some other time it will all turn out.
This is it. No one else has the answer.
No other place will be better, and it has already turned out.
At the centre of our being you have the answer;
you know who you are and you know what you want.
There is no need to run outside for better seeing.
Nor peer from a window.
Rather abide at the centre of your being;
for the more you leave it, the less you learn.
Search your heart and see the way to do is to be.

– LAO TSE

Practise uncertainty

Cartoonist Bill Watterson once said this great line: "Reality continues to ruin my life." How many of us feel exactly the same way? Well, I would be happy and successful if life wouldn't always get in my way. The great thing is: Life will always be 'in your way', there will always be bumps in the road, life will always take unexpected turns, and light and darkness will always alternate each other. Even better: most of the time it's not up to us to decide what we want, and, usually, things are far beyond our own comprehension – they simply happen. That's life; it teaches us the amazing power of grace.

*

By letting go you no longer hold back life.

*

But we are not very adventurous creatures, we are not very fond of uncertainty. We prefer security and strive for it throughout our lives. We constantly want to know what comes next in life. We only feel good and safe in our lives when we can plan ahead and understand fully what takes place or what's going to take place. When we cannot, we freak out. Which really isn't a surprise. We aren't trained in how to handle uncertainty and change, because no one teaches us that, although they are the foundations of life. Our upbringing and education focuses on teaching us how to get a grip on life, how we can plan and influence our future.

But how much more valuable would it be if, from a very early age, we were taught how to deal with change? Change is inherent in our earthly existence. Control and certainty are by definition always temporary and nothing more than an illusion created by the mind: the illusion of self-sustainability.

In recent decades we've been busy with wanting more, accomplishing more and making more money. Power, social status and money play increasingly bigger roles in our lives. But in the meantime, we have everything we want and yet it's still not enough.

*

Letting go is the most important code of the New Age.

*

During my readings around the country, I continually come across people whose lives are exactly as they had once wanted and planned them to be: a nice job, nice house, good car, two kids and four holidays per year. But at the end of yet another hurried and stressful day we find ourselves unhappy in our oh-so-perfect lives. Many people discover that the so-called control is only an illusion and that they still don't experience any inner peace, despite the perfection they believe they have created. They miss the connection with their own soul and haven't been able to be fully present or to experience any joy.

That is the price we pay for the illusion that happiness is feasible and that you can achieve anything if you put your mind to it. It is a nerve-racking way to live life, which seems to break people apart. I see that people are deliberately slowing things down in order to create more space for better quality in life. More and more people are moving away from striving for more and are consciously choosing less, to be satisfied with what they have and not have a continuous desire for more.

We must try to fix reality, but be satisfied with what we have; a transition from always doing to doing less, travelling from the outside world to our inner world, from the illusion of separation to oneness, from mastering to surrendering, from overfull day planners to more silence, emptiness and rest. Many people (especially those of us in our forties) look back and see that their 'iron will' didn't bring them the peace and happiness that they desired, and shift into a more 'relaxed will'. We are starting to understand that we don't have to become something because we are already something, that we don't have to find anything because everything is already here. Letting go is the most important code of the New Age.

An exercise in letting go

These days, we are so quick to say, 'Oh, you should just let that go'. But how do you do that? Start with this small exercise. Are you one of those people that is stuck in doing mode, instead of being mode? Are you racing to get from point A to B, without stopping to smell the roses? Then put an end to all that running and rushing, starting right now. Stop planning four appointments in one night and consciously choose to do just one thing. The next step is to let go of the future and the past and to be fully present in the here and now. What do you see? What do you feel? What do you smell? It may seem like a simple exercise. But just try it. You will experience that more rest enters your system, your stress will lessen, you will start to feel more energetic and clear-sighted, and your quality of life will expand.

Buddhism

I have always found the Buddhist teachings on letting go the most beautiful and clearest to me. A Buddhist teacher once said: 'Letting go means getting a lot of peace and letting go of it all, it means experiencing total peace.' I imagine that most of you haven't seen the beautiful documentary *Buddha's Lost Children* by Dutch director Mark Verkerk, but I highly recommend it. What an amazing movie! It is about a former Thai boxer Samerchai, who becomes a Buddhist monk. He is given the name Phra Khru Bah and was the founder of the Monastery of the Temple of the Golden Horse, where he accommodates children and animals.

*

*Letting go means getting a lot of peace and letting go of it all;
it means experiencing total peace.*

*

Every child that comes to live in the Temple of the Golden Horse is given a horse. Often, these children are severely traumatized when they arrive, but by giving them the responsibility of caring for their own horse, they learn to form a bond; at first with the animal, but later also with people. The children do everything with these horses: the documentary shows us beautiful images of the young monks swimming together with their trusted new friends.

There is a breathtaking scene in this documentary about 'letting go'. At one point little A-thee's horse dies. The young monk is inconsolable as he cries and sits next to the dead horse; he cuts a piece of the horse's mane to keep as a reminder. His teacher explains to him that what he is going through is the most important Buddhist lesson there is: embracing the continuous progress, renewal and therefore understanding the instability of life. It is so touching how he explains it to the boy.

Buddhism shows us so beautifully that when we deprive ourselves of our life's breath, we are out of kilter with the fleetingness of our earthly existence and the perishability of all material things. Reconciling ourselves with that reality is our soul's assignment during our earthly life.

Is letting go the same as passivity – a downplaying or suppression of things?

Whether it is about letting go of something outside of ourselves or inside of ourselves, the principle remains the same: it's about giving up your dependency. For what purpose? To offer space to being fully present and living a real and honest life. Is this a passive or fatalistic attitude? Of course not, on the contrary.

Real courage and stamina is demanded from us to travel the road inward. During moments of unrest, utter chaos, exhaustion and depression, it takes real discipline to continually figure out where you are putting the blocks to your own life and not functioning from a place of total acceptance. It takes an enormous amount of discipline to constantly and sincerely want whatever presents itself and not to enter into a discussion with reality.

That really is a very different type of discipline to the one we learn from a lot of New Age thinking and meaning: that we have to work hard on ourselves first in order to find happiness, that everything should be better and different because we have so dramatically lost our way. This is a huge misconception. I have written it before, but I cannot repeat it enough: spirituality is not about working on yourself or improving yourself.

Living consciously or spiritually (or whatever you would like to call it) is not a question of controlling your feelings or thoughts. No, only one thing is important here: to always and in every moment consciously and without any resistance offer space to reality. Your life will become real again, there is room for reality; so, go easy, step back, many problems will disappear like snow in the sun. Why? Because by accepting what is, you take away the barriers that are blocking the natural flow of your life. In short: an accepting, releasing type of attitude is anything but passive, but rather a very real and dynamic attitude.

Is letting go the same as suppressing, denying or downplaying certain things within yourself? No, it's not. An example: unpleasant emotions like fear, anger, frustration and sadness usually bring up a particular resistance in us. We don't want to know that we have them, and we don't want to feel them. A lot of people confuse suppressing or burying with the concept of letting go, but when you push away your feelings, it doesn't mean they are out of your system. Sooner or later they will come back to the surface. That's why it's so important to truly let go of these types of emotions.

*

You let go by actually allowing a particular feeling in.

*

Don't downplay feelings or emotions, don't deny them, but simply let them be without judgement. Keep them coming. Don't identify yourself with negativity. You are not that anger or sadness. They are just emotions that come and go, all they do is point out your soul's desire. They are like soul roadmaps. Experience and observe them and afterwards ask yourself if you can let them go, want to let them go and, if so, when? If you can answer the first two questions with 'yes' easily, you will notice that things change almost instantaneously.

So, you're saying to yourself, 'Nothing about me needs to be denied.' This, too, is allowed to be here, this, too, is part of me right now. I am letting it go, it doesn't mean: I want to get rid of the feeling. No, 'I let it go' means that you release your judgement about that feeling. Just drop that judgement about your emotions, the same way you drop a piece of paper on the floor. Allow yourself to be a whole human being, with all its positive and negative sides that are intrinsic to all human beings. Light and darkness together form the whole. Should one half of yourself be allowed to be here but not the other? Trying to manage that will cost you a great deal of energy.

*

Don't wish to let go of the painful emotions, but let go of the fight against them.

*

After all, you're not half of you but a complete person. A whole and total package. You weren't born to be perfect, enlightened or holy, but to become a complete human being! So by giving that feeling permission to be there, it loses its sabotaging and destructive power. So don't let go by wishing to get rid of it, but by actually allowing a certain feeling in. That is the only way your shadow side loses its power. You're not suppressing it, but putting it in the light: it's allowed to be here!

Recognize your shadow side, acknowledge and accept it and then dismantle it. You know that what you fight against will grow and increase in power. So don't wish to let go of the painful emotions, but rather to let go of the fight against them. But especially let go of the need to want! While we are at it, you may as well do that right now. Experience what happens. What does letting go bring you?

Learning to let go has everything to do with learning to surrender. It is said 'He who argues with reality argues with God'. It is about allowing reality into your world, offering space to reality – every moment, over and over again. To be open to everything there is, without resistance or judgement. If there is one thing I have learned – and I've written this before – it is that the biggest changes will take place when you no longer fight against what is.

*

He who argues with reality argues with God.

*

Learning to let go will bring you significant changes, it has an enormous healing power, and it will bring a great release into your life. What if, for a whole week, you consciously choose to offer no resistance to whatever comes your way and to what you experience? You will find that beautiful changes will take place. Problems seem to disappear (because if you've let go of all your judgements, then there are actually no problems), you will feel better in your own skin, more energetic and look better. People will respond differently to you. You will experience all kinds of interesting coincidences and find that a lot of things are suddenly easier. That is because you have an open and accepting attitude which takes away anything blocking your energy and allows it to flow freely.

*

You don't practise letting go, you just do it.

*

By letting go, you no longer hold back your own life. When you stop wanting to change, stop controlling and dominating everything that happens, you will notice the resistance around you disappears and problems resolve on their own. Let go of all the concepts and ideas you have of yourself, your life, life itself, your body and of others. See, feel, smell and taste life as it is right now.

Deepak Chopra said it beautifully: "Enjoy each moment, no matter what the outcome will be. That is living in the wisdom of uncertainty." It's not as scary as it sounds, but at some point you just have to decide to do it. The moment you let go of control and completely enter reality, you will begin to experience life in a whole new way.

What are some practical ways to learn to let go?

1. Start to breathe consciously.
2. Surrender control: relinquish your role as manager of the universe.
3. Trust that you will be taken care of when you let go of control.
4. Realize that you are fine just as you are and that everything is as it should be for a very good reason.
5. Don't keep life at a distance with rationalizations.
6. Delete the word 'but' from your vocabulary.
7. Don't criticize, but accept.

Summary

1} We have no experience in how to handle uncertainty and change, because no one teaches us how, even though this is the foundation of life.

2} Our upbringing and education teaches us how to get a grip on life, how we can plan and influence our future. But it would be far more valuable if, starting at a young age, it would teach us how to cope with change.

3} Change is imminent in our earthly existence. Control and security are by definition temporary and nothing more than an illusion created by the mind.

4} Many people (especially those in their forties) look back at life and see that their 'iron will' did not bring them the quality of life they were searching for and decide to shift towards a more relaxed type of attitude.

5} Letting go is the most important code of the New Age.

6} By letting go, you no longer hold back on your life.

7} When you stop wanting to change, control and dominate everything that happens, you will notice the resistance around you disappears and problems resolve on their own.

embracing
the mystery

The real trick to life is not to be in the know,
but to be in the mystery.

– FRED ALAN WOLF

Accepting the dance

Embracing the mystery is almost the same as letting go and
obviously they are connected. But they are not exactly the same
thing, so therefore I would like to elaborate on it a bit more. You
see, embracing the mystery takes letting go one step further. It's
not possible to get ahead of the unexpected events in our lives,
and we never really know when or how our lives will change;
that's a good thing, because that is precisely the essence of our

earthly journey. It is one big invitation to 'accept the dance', without any guarantees and security, without wanting to know where this dance will lead or how long it will last.

We will never be able to wrap our brains around the mystery anyway. In the same inexplicable way, life started once long ago. Respect and love for the mystery are key to learning how to make peace with your human 'being' and with your earthly existence. If you continue to always want and need to understand everything, then you have a big problem.

*

Life is not a conspiracy against you
but a conspiracy to help you.

*

There are those moments in life where you simply have no other choice but to surrender all control. You know what? Those are the really sacred moments! They are opportunities to experience pure dedication and deep initiation that takes you to the secret space within yourself where everything is good. We all know that when we experience utter desperation, it usually leads us to a real turning point in our lives. Over the years, I've spoken to so many people who, just like me, were forced to their knees by life's difficulties, forcing them, in turn, to travel the road inward and find a solution inward rather than finding one in the outside world.

In my own life I have noticed that just when you find yourself in the great unknown, at your most desperate, that is when the answer comes. Maybe because in those moments the thinking mind is finally silenced, it gives in because it is out of options and solutions, and the real 'knowledge' within you finally has a chance to take over. Each time life takes away our security and safety, it offers us a chance to surrender. Loss, in whatever form, gives birth to trust.

My connection to the secret

Does all of this sound like abstract mumbo jumbo to you? Then look at it like this: don't you think that the strength and power that manages to hold together entire galaxies and parallel universes would also be able to take care of you? That you're just a meaningless little ant on this big earth and that all those universal and natural laws simply don't apply to you? We are not spectators on the sidelines, watching the enormous power of life; we are an intricate part of that mystic force field, no matter how hard we want to believe we are not, no matter how much we think we're above it all.

*

I experience the respect and honour I have for the secret of it all as healing on a very deep level.

*

The choice to surrender to that power is up to us. Sometimes it's very easy for us. But: do you know when? When it concerns unimportant things, things that don't matter so much to us anyway. Those things we will just leave up to God. In those moments we are courageous and we dare to trust in the deeper powers of life. But when it really matters, we think we need to intervene and direct, and that it's better if we resolve it ourselves, not God. However, if you dare, precisely during those challenging moments, to surrender all of your control, you will find that you are totally taken care of. You will find that life is not a conspiracy against you but rather a conspiracy to help you.

I have always had a deep connection to this secret. There really was no other choice for me, because starting at a very young age, so many unexplainable things happened to me in succession. The urge to understand why the things happened to me as they did in a very natural way made room for a kind of primal trust in the higher order of all things, something that transcends all of our rational thinking. How did that happen? I have no idea. It feels like my soul entered this world with this deep sense of trust. I'm thankful for it, because when we speak about healing and any cure, in any form, two of the most disempowering questions are: How? and Why?

*

Our need to know is part of our survival instinct.

*

Are they understandable questions? Yes. Our need to know is part of our survival instinct, especially when it comes to the events which happen to us that determine and affect the rest of our lives, like my own disability, for instance. We think that if life offers us an instruction manual for these events, it is easier to carry out our fate. Because if we don't have that manual to tell us the how and why, we are left with feelings such as: What did I do to deserve this, what did I do wrong? What negative thinking patterns in me caused this to happen? What did I miss or overlook? Most people think that when they figure out this part, they can eliminate the source of the illness and that, in return, they will be rewarded with good health. Certainly, that could happen, but it's not usually the case. It is never the goal of the soul to become better or recover physically. The soul's only goal is to grow.

The belief system of good and bad

It's possible that due to undergoing a crisis, you experience an enormous amount of growth and, at the same time, manage to recover physically; one certainly doesn't exclude the other. But in order to move beyond the suffering, we must stop questioning and asking why, and look deeper into the belief system behind the thought that bad things shouldn't happen to good people.

Many people share and apply this belief to situations. "They are such good people, why did they have a disabled child?" Well, my parents were also beautiful, loving people and they still had a daughter with a disability. My husband is a caring, responsible, compassionate man who, despite all his purity and goodness, still lost his 17-year-old daughter in the tsunami in Thailand.

Holding on to the belief system of 'good or bad' only leads to pain and stagnation. The first step in order to make space for any kind of healing is to let go of the urge to know why things happen as they do. Is this difficult? Yes, of course it is. Letting go of belief systems, patterns and convictions is more difficult than giving up our attachments to shopping, smoking or eating fatty foods. But it is incredibly important, because hanging on to that urge to know means hanging on to the pain.

*

To make space for healing we have to let go of our urge to know why things happen as they do.

*

Ultimately, it's about being able to see loss, misfortune or disease as a crisis that wants to open our eyes to reality and, at the same time, wants to offer us the chance to get closer to ourselves and to God – or the mystery of the universe. That healing, or not healing, isn't really all that important, but that it's about whether we take on the inner challenge that the illness or disability brought us, that we discover what secret desire our soul has hidden behind this illness.

You cannot reason with illness or crisis

It is not all that important to me to know how and why I have this spinal cord injury. I cannot tell you how many times I have heard: Why don't you do another Lyme disease test? Most people cannot fathom the thought that the absence of a clear explanation for my disability doesn't make me uncomfortable. Actually, the opposite is true: the deep respect I have for the secret of it brings me peace. I experience this as a mystical act and experience it as healing on a very deep level. Besides, whether I know or do not know what the cause is doesn't change the fact that I still have (and want) to deal with it. It's my choice not to demand an explanation from life, or the universe, but to give my own value, meaning and purpose to events.

*

I am free to give my own value or meaning to something if it feels right and good to me.

*

This is what it truly means to me to have control in life: I am free to give my own value or meaning to something, if it feels right and good to me. That is true personal sustainability. Our fight against the crisis, in whatever form, is usually quite rough until we respect the secret behind it and become our own meaningful answer to the events. So most of the time it's not about searching for the meaning of the events, but rather to experience that we can do something else with these events and give them our own meaning. Consciousness development has nothing to do with finding the 'perfect fit' answers and solutions, but with how we look at ourselves. The basis of healing is a complete acceptance of yourself and your situation, even if you no longer rationally understand yourself or the situation.

Soul planning
It is important to learn to trust our soul when it comes to its choices. Those familiar with my way of thinking know that I believe in 'soul planning'. I am convinced that we plan the challenges we face in our life before our birth, that they are the conscious choices our soul makes to further our spiritual growth

and that everything happens to remind us of who we really are. Our soul makes certain choices before we return to earth (and also during our lifetime here) and has a life plan mapped out for us, mainly from a desire to learn from new experiences and to grow. The consequences of those choices aren't always fun, but they are a real part of the journey towards our spiritual growth.

*

The soul makes certain choices before we return to earth.

*

The soul doesn't see things as right or wrong and doesn't think in time. It is always aware of its own immortality, but its only real concern is growth; it has no attachment to what amount of time is needed for it. The soul sees a crisis, illness or disability not as a failure or punishment. It doesn't know judgement, it doesn't label events or situations in a dualistic manner, like our personality conscious does. To the soul, every experience is an opportunity for healing and growth.

But don't just take my word for it. Ask yourself this: With everything that has happened in your life, or is happening at the moment, can you imagine that your soul planned this experience before your birth? Why would your soul have done this? What is it trying to accomplish? By asking yourself these questions, the challenges in your life will have a different charge on them and, most likely, give it a whole different meaning. By approaching things in this way, you will travel a completely new road, a road which offers you a lot more loving space for everything that happens in our lives.

Summary

1} Respect and love for the mystery is the key to making peace with your own human 'being' and your earthly existence.

2} If you always need to understand everything with your mind, then you really have a problem.

3} Our need to know is part of our survival instinct, especially when it comes to situations that could determine the rest of our lives.

4} You cannot reason with illness or crisis.

5} In order to make space for healing, the first thing we have to do is give up our urge to know why things happen as they do.

6} Is that difficult? Yes, of course it is. Letting go of belief systems, patterns and convictions is more difficult than giving up your attachment to clothes, shopping or eating fatty foods.

7} It is incredibly important we do this, because holding on to our urge to know means holding on to the pain.

8} Honouring the power of the secret is a mystical act; it offers us peace and healing on a very deep level.

becoming your own answer

*God is omnipresent [...] God is present in every situation –
no matter how difficult it is.*

– FATHER TITUS BRANDSMA

Accepting the unacceptable

If you haven't seen the film *The Living Matrix*, I highly recommend it. It's truly a groundbreaking film about the entirely new, scientific point of view on healing. Scientists, physiologists and bioenergetics researchers share their vision, knowledge and experience and their theories behind the seemingly miraculous cure that some of the people that you meet in the documentary have experienced. From the quantum physics of the body field to informative medicine, the film looks at and introduces new and innovative ideas about health and how these ideas will influence our well-being, healing process and medicine as a whole in the near future.

*

How do we react when we have nothing left to hold on to?

*

I was especially touched by Arielle Essex's life story, a beautiful young woman diagnosed with a large tumour in her head. Hers is also a story about redefining the concept of healing. From the moment she found out she had this tumour, all the walls of safety and security in her life fell apart. However, that's exactly when life starts to become really interesting. Because what do we do when we no longer know where we stand and find ourselves in a total free fall in our life? How do we react when we have nothing left to hold on to? It is interesting to think about what we thought we were holding on to to begin with? Where do we land inside ourselves when we fall? I find it truly interesting, hopeful and comforting to see and hear the stories of people who – for whatever reason – have stood eye to eye with the grimness of our earthly existence and then did something positive with that experience. They're not people who need justification or who demand an answer from life, but people who became the answer to the questions and challenges in their own lives.

*

A huge tumour in your head: is that fair?

*

Arielle Essex is one of those people. Her story is not only beautiful, but also her experience and the way she connects things and puts them into words touched me deeply. Arielle's journey is a striking example of the underlying perfection and logic of what we may perceive as the universe's seemingly huge 'mistakes' or giant 'errors'. A huge tumour in your head: is that fair? Or is that not what it's about? Does this illness have a meaning? If so, what does it mean? If not, why not? Is it possible to accept this monster residing in your head? Is the fact that you get something like this proof of the existence of God and of a higher order, or is this actually the ultimate proof of its absence?

Coincidence or reason?

Arielle's story is a personal journey through – among other things – these questions. In her own words, she "desperately" wanted to have children. It was even the reason why she divorced her husband; she wanted to have children and he did not. So she moved to London, thinking that it would take her a maximum of two years to find a new partner and settle down. In her mind she had the whole thing worked out: "I'd be out living in the country, having my 2.5 children, and I'd be totally happy. That was the plan."

*

Is an illness like this proof of the existence of God and of a higher order, or is it actually the ultimate proof of its absence?

*

"I was very good at making plans. So there I was," she says in the documentary. "I had my osteopathic practice, and I was seeing clients. And I was stressed, frustrated and depressed." Arielle soon discovered, in a very big way, how the plans that we make in our head often don't coincide with the plans our soul has in store for us during this lifetime. She'd been having headaches for well over ten years that only seemed to be getting worse. During a routine visit, the doctor found her hormone levels to be completely out of balance, and he immediately suspected that she might have a tumour. She was sent for a brain scan where a prolactinoma (a tumour in the pituitary gland) was found. Obviously, this was a big shock to her, and at first she thought: "How unfair!" She researched this type of tumour and read every book on the subject. She says: "When I discovered that it caused infertility, I thought: that is so ironic. Every cell in my body was saying I want children and I had somehow created a tumour that stopped me from having children. There had to be some reason for this, there had to be, this was too much of a coincidence."

Arielle became very curious, and because of her alternative medicine background, she decided to treat this alternatively, rather than through orthodox drugs or surgery. She decided to utilize NLP (neuro-linguistic programming) to approach her tumour. When she applied this on a much deeper level, she made some very interesting discoveries. "Now, remember, I was the person who thought every cell in her body wanted children. But what I discovered was that deep down going back to my early childhood, I had such abhorrence of what my family had been like, that the last thing in the world part of me wanted was to be a mother. This really, really shocked me. I thought I wanted one thing, and, in fact, an unconscious part of me was going in a completely different direction [...] It helped me understand why I had created a life that didn't go down that path."

*

*If I am attacking my tumour with all those thoughts of wanting to get rid of it, that's murderous!
That cannot be healing.*

*

One day, she heard a little voice shouting inside her head: "I'm so sick of this. I just want to be rid of this whole nightmare;

I want to be rid of this tumour!" She was shocked at the amount of anger and frustration inside of her and thought: "That's a lot of self-attack. If I am attacking my tumour with all those thoughts of wanting to get rid of it, that's murderous! That cannot be healing." She goes on to explain that she had never looked at healing in this way. She realized that every thought she'd had was about getting rid of it and that this was obviously a huge inner conflict. She decided to have a closer look at it and thought: "What would be the opposite? It has to be acceptance." She goes on to say: "What would it be like if I really accepted this tumour?"

Tumour as a guide

A few years later, there was a turning point in her recovery when she realized that her tumour had taken her on a journey she had never planned. It had taught her things she had never intended to learn. She had changed her career and her whole outlook and had learned so much about herself and others. She says: "I had experiences I'd never had before. I met amazing people, wonderful people, from all over the world. I'd had the support of people all over the world. And I realized I liked myself a lot better. And so I thought, OK, I can see that this tumour hasn't been totally bad. What if it has a purpose or a reason for being here? Obviously, it's done a good job so far. So if it has a purpose for being here, maybe there's still a purpose? What would happen if I gave it permission to stay for the rest of my life?"

*

I thought: What would it be like if
I really accepted this tumour?

*

Six months after she'd had that realization, she began to fully accept the presence of her tumour. She went for her routine blood test with her specialist, and to her surprise her hormone levels were completely normal. Her doctor couldn't believe it. She thought there may have been a mistake, that the blood test reading was wrong. She thought, 'Well, I'm older now, maybe my hormones have changed.' But the doctor reassured her that was not possible. He told her it could only mean one thing: that her tumour was gone and that this was a real credit to her attitude. "I don't know how you did it, or what you did," he said, "but I have to tell you I've been seeing you for ten years and you're not the same person you were ten years ago, you are completely different."

I was so happy with her contribution to this movie. There was nothing abstract or new-agey about her story, there was no abracadabra effect. It just showed us in a simple and personal way that an unbelievable healing power is released when we lovingly open up to the unacceptable and the unthinkable, if we dare say a wholehearted 'yes' to all that happens in reality.

Summary

1} Arielle Essex found she had a tumour in her head. What happened to her afterwards is a shining example of the underlying perfection or logic of seemingly big mistakes or errors the universe makes.

2} She discovered that her tumour made her infertile. She found that to be ironic. "Every cell in my body wanted children, and somehow I created a tumour that made this impossible. There had to be a reason, it was too much of a coincidence."

3} She came to realize that deep inside, because of her experience in youth, she was so horrified about her family life that the last thing an unconscious part of her wanted was to be a mother. This really shocked her. So she thought she wanted one thing, but an unconscious part of her was going in a completely different direction.

4} One day, she realized that spending all her time trying to get rid of the tumour could never be healing. That this caused a huge inner conflict.

5} She decided to accept her tumour. Better still, she gave it permission to stay for the rest of her life.

6} Six months after this realization, she began to truly accept the presence of her tumour, and a blood test done by her specialist showed that her hormone levels had returned to normal. The tumour had disappeared.

consciousness over matter

A thing is complete when you can let it be.

– GITA BELLIN

Experiment

Because of a move I ended up being treated by exactly the same physiotherapist (acupuncturist and orthomolecular doctor) who had also treated me as a teenager, 23 years earlier. After a few initial examinations, he smiled at me and said he would love to have me examined by a Vitascanner, to see how my overall health was, after spending over 30 years in that wheelchair. For those of you not familiar with this method, Vitascanning is a computer-controlled, bioenergetic, diagnostic and medical device based on so-called informative medicine. This device, developed by scientists, makes it possible to very accurately and reliably measure your general overall health and shows your weak spots. I found the whole idea a little scary, because the scan can show you everything, literally everything, going on in your body. Every bacteria, every little parasite can be measured with this device. Did I really want or need to know all of that?

*

The body isn't built or designed for a lifetime of sitting.

*

But curiosity got the best of me, and I decided to do it anyway. I thought I should probably be concerned about the state of my body after so many years in a wheelchair, right? Or not? Actually, I wasn't sure. I felt great, energetic and clear, and I didn't have the feeling that I should be concerned about anything at all. But you never know. The body isn't built or designed for a lifetime of sitting. I thought about the fellow paraplegic people I know who have been in a wheelchair for as long as I have, and most of them had their share of related health issues. So, an overall health check may not be such a bad idea, and I went ahead with it. Besides, I thought it would make for quite an interesting experiment. How were those bones doing after so many years of lack of pressure? What were the consequences of a disrupted blood circulation? And what about my heart and blood vessels?

*

*Every bacteria, every little parasite can be measured
with this device. Did I really want or need
to know all of that?*

*

Filled with curiosity, I sat down. What if I'd been wrong? I could hardly imagine it, but who knows? Before the scan started, I promised myself quickly to be 'in the moment' in case something unexpected or confronting was discovered, and then we started. During the next two hours I watched as body parts passed by one after the other. From my brain to my ears, eyes, jaw, teeth, spine, joints, organs, skin, bones and down to the blood vessels. If green and pink spots were to appear, it was a good thing – however, red and black triangles would show points in need of attention or of real concern.

And what do you know? Nearly everything coloured serenely pink and green! We were both quite surprised. I was ridiculously healthy. "I don't know how you're doing it, how it's possible that after so many years of sitting, you're still so vital and energetic. But you're doing it!" my therapist said. "You're way above average compared to most of the people I measure here. With you, it's obviously a case of mind over matter, there is no other explanation other than that your attitude in life contributes to your health and physical well-being." But I wondered, was it mind over matter, or was it heart over matter? Or both? We create with our whole consciousness, with our way of thinking and feeling, we create who we are. That power is undeniably a vastly greater authority than the physical one.

Whenever I give lectures to groups of my peers, there is always someone in the audience who gets up (remarkably often an attendant or caregiver for someone with a disability) that says something along the lines of: "Yeah, easy for you to say. You have self-confidence, self-esteem, you are intelligent, you have talent, and you look nice." My answer is always: "No. There really is only one real difference between myself and many other people (with or without restrictions): I am in a total and complete calm state of acceptance, and that is the foundation of my strength and my health."

Spectator and participant

Am I always in that calm state of acceptance? Of course not! Life has been – as it has for most of us – very difficult for me at times;

from an early age I was faced with great challenges, to which I also didn't have a quick or proper response, and even resisted those challenges with all my might. Those of you who have read some of my other books know that, for example, my mother died at a very young age. I was a teenager when it happened and struggled with it for years. I had such a stress reaction that all my hair fell out. I also experienced great disappointments in my love life, and in those moments I really didn't think, 'Oh well, let's just quickly accept all of that and move on!'

*

When you can no longer do what you want to do,
you have to learn to want what you are able to do.

*

As I grew older – like most people who become older and learn something along the way – I obviously learned to take some distance when faced with difficult situations, and to look at the situation more as a spectator rather than a participant. If you can teach yourself during moments of chaos to get off the stage of life and have a seat in the audience with a bucket of popcorn and a nice blanket, you will discover that you can choose to make a big or small emotional drama out of your existence.

But when it comes to my own disability, I was never really panicked or confused about it from the start. It didn't take long after I became ill before a natural, deep and calm acceptance came over me. I didn't have to do anything brilliant to accomplish that. It's just the way it was. I always felt that this belonged to me and to my journey in this life. It gave me a deep feeling of ease and relaxation in my life, and allowed me to have a great deal of resilience, both physically and mentally. This type of primal trust and acceptance are, to me, the real forces behind my immune system, my consciousness and body.

*

Frustration comes from resisting 'what is'.

*

Does accepting my own disability mean it never bothers me? Do I never think where I live in the country, in these beautiful surroundings – damn, I wish I could take a hike with my dogs in the woods through all those impossible little trails and paths? Of course I do. I harbour those feelings as well. They are also part of me. Because my handicap absolutely limits me, it makes me unable to do a lot of things, and I live a very different life to most walking, completely healthy women. Of course I fully experience these limitations as limitations, which sometimes make my life impossible. Most of the time, my mind is way ahead of my body and my body says, 'No, I'm taking time out.' But, in a way, this may also be my saviour.

Giving up resistance

I know I've written this before, but I think it's important to repeat it: this body 'forces' me to stay close to myself and my thoughts and to focus on what I feel I am meant to do here, to focus on what is really important in my life. I do not experience my body as sabotaging my quality of life but as my servant. It's been my experience that the worst thing we can do when faced with pain is to try and gain control over something we can never gain control of. I am generally healthy, but I do have a body that experiences pain daily. I need more than your average care and attention, and it asks me to be extremely attentive.

*

'Za' means: to sit without movement, like a mountain.
'Zen' means: to understand the essence of the universe.

*

Pain is a given fact in my life. It would be hard to imagine how it could not be. Just close your eyes. In your mind place yourself in a chair and imagine being forced to stay there for years. Not for a few hours or for a day. No, for more than 30 years. It doesn't take a lot to realize that this cannot be good for a body, it's simply not built or designed for it. Yet my situation is a fact and every passing moment gives me a choice: do I resist it or do I surrender to it?

*

If we really want control, then we should let go
of the illusion that control exists.

*

I chose the latter at an early age. Not consciously, because I was too young for that. I think my soul knew from the start: the body will do what it wants anyway, just let it go, and meanwhile I will go on living my life. I never had a strong identification with my body. After all, I am not my body, but I have a body. I treat it gently and lovingly, but I don't try and force my will on it and prefer to find out what direction it is pointing me in.

I don't see my body, with all its imperfections, as the enemy, but more as an ally. My body is my Zen master, whether I want it to be or not. I once read this piece and have kept it in my day planner ever since:

What Zen is all about:
The Zen student said to his master: "What is this sitting all about?"
The master said: "To get you to wonder what it is all about."
The student said: "Well, then it really succeeded."
A little later the student asked: "So what is all that wondering all about?"
The master answered: "To let you feel what it is like not to have an answer."

The student said: "Well, then it really succeeded."
A little later the student asked: "So what is that feeling to not have the answer all about?"
The master answered: "To show you what Zen is all about."
The student said: "Well, then it really failed."
The master answered: "You better continue to sit."
The student said: "But then what is Zen all about?"
The master answered: "If I knew, I would not be your master."

To sit in 'zazen' is the basis of Zen Buddhism: to sit without judgement, without striving for something, without a goal. 'Za' means: to sit without movement, like a mountain. 'Zen' means: concentration, understanding the essence of the universe. Zen is simply to sit. To sit without motive, without a goal, without trying to accomplish anything. How beautiful is that, really? It's not necessary for me to retreat to a Japanese monastery to experience the Zen teachings because I have experienced these teachings daily in their purest form for well over 30 years from my own body!

Your body is your own personal Zen master

Whether they are big or small, we all receive the lessons our body wants to teach us at the exact right and suitable moment, time and place and in just the right form. It is important we stop taking them personally and to start recognizing the message. What lessons and clues do you receive from your body? When something happens, try to see and feel past the personal. That way, you take the drama and heaviness out of the equation, and you can focus on an entirely different kind of healing.

Don't forget: all your experiences are part of a greater reality. By placing them in a broader perspective – both positive and negative – you will gain insight into the deeper meaning of it. Now that's something you can really use. By looking at it in this way, your problems aren't always just difficult situations that you must get rid of as soon as possible, but also as a chance for development and growth.

*

When something happens,
try to see and feel past the personal.

*

It is so valuable to recognize this Zen factor in the events of our lives. Try replacing the question 'What is life taking away from me?' with the question 'What is this experience bringing me and what can I learn from it?' You can really renew yourself and find more depth in your life. Fear, pain and grief – sooner or later we will all experience them. And if during those moments we really want control, then we should start by letting go of the illusion that control even exists. Feel and experience the pain with every cell in your body and allow it to be your own personal Zen master. Undergo, endure what the body does or doesn't do, without thinking about it too much. When you're sick, be sick and nothing more. You can help or support your body, but fighting against it is no foundation for any kind of healing in any form. Let your rational approach go; your body knows what it's doing. Any illness is an opportunity to become reconnected to reality. Surrender yourself to reality, without a motive, without a goal and especially without an attachment to a particular outcome.

Summary

1} Our body is our own Zen master.

2} The lessons our body teaches us take place at exactly the right moment, place and time, and precisely in the right form.

3} Sooner or later we all experience fear, pain and grief. And if, during those moments, we really want control, then we should start by letting go of the illusion that control even exists.

4} It is also very important to stop taking events in our life personally.

5} When something happens, try to see and feel past the personal. That way, you take the drama and heaviness out of the equation, and you can focus on an entirely different kind of healing.

6} Remember that all your experiences are part of a greater reality.

7} By placing your experiences in a broader perspective – both positive and negative – you will gain insight into the deeper meaning of it.

8} By looking at it in this way, your problems aren't always just difficult situations that you must get rid of as soon as possible, but also as a chance for development and growth.

8

how we create reality

Embracing reality with gratitude is
an act of regeneration.

– THE DEEPER SECRET

What is your basic attitude in life?
Both Arielle Essex's life story and mine show us that our consciousness has an unbelievable influence on the chemistry in our body, and that the way we feel in our own skin mirrors our consciousness. We have known this for a long time, but the world of regular medicine is now slowly starting to catch up as well. What is also an important question: what is your basic attitude towards the events happening in your life? All conceivable emotions only have two sources: love or fear. You could also say: trust or distrust. Love is relaxing for your body; fear is stress for the body. Trust is surrendering to the

flow of life; distrust is resistance to the flow of life. Love is constructive; fear is destructive. Trust is constructive; distrust is undermining.

*

Experiencing love is relaxing for your body;
experiencing fear is stressful for the body.

*

It is crucial to your health to feel at home and safe in your own life, or whether you are on good terms with the reality of this moment or if you're resisting it. To feel safe and rooted in life, to feel self-respect and self-worth – they all contribute to a sense of great ease and relaxation on a deep level in your life. We can see this type of relaxation in our facial expression, posture, our body language and in the way we move. It has also been demonstrated scientifically that it plays a crucial part in the creation of other hormones and the electric control of our central nervous system. To be on good terms with the sometimes grim reality of our earthly life and to trust in the deeper forces of life is obviously much more than an attitude alone. It is not only a psychological phenomenon or a sound spiritual attitude. No, it has actually been demonstrated to be highly effective in stimulating the immune system and the self-healing capacity of our body. Over the past few years it has been scientifically proven that it is a misconception to think that this is about an exclusive psychological state.

What is your basic emotional state?
Do your core thoughts and emotions find their origin in love and trust or in fear and distrust? In the next few days, or weeks, see from what inner source you are naturally inclined to react to things. What is your basic attitude towards events? What is your basic emotional state?

The power of emotions and thoughts

When the conscience changes, the body changes with it. When you renew yourself by leaving your comfort zone, when you replace your old way of thinking with a new way and when you make the effort to imagine a positive development, then everything in and around you will eventually change with you as well. Every cell in your body is aware of what your brain is thinking, of your mood changes and of your deepest convictions. Our body is ruled by our consciousness. If it changes, then the whole energy of our body will change. New science has shown us that you can even change your genes in this way.

*

We never become stressed by something outside of ourselves, but only by what happens inside of us.

*

Emotions and thoughts are powerful creative instruments, and we are constantly finding new ways to consciously apply this power as a useful tool. But don't think: 'I want to accept reality with all of my being right now, because then I will quickly get what I want, then I will heal this condition I have, or then I will live longer.' Because that's not the way it works. Acceptance means to fully embrace what is. Without reservation, without ifs and buts, without a goal, without an attachment to a result. Take Arielle Essex, for example. Her goal was not to become 'better', but to embrace her condition, as a real part of her life and as a guide, and to bury the hatchet and end the battle: "OK, tumour, since you're there no matter what I think or do, show me why you are here." Once she embraced the tumour and felt that peace, the tumour's mission was complete.

Don't think, 'Oh, so acceptance is a guarantee for healing', because then you have misunderstood me. What I do know from my own experience is that, just like Arielle Essex, to fight what happens never leads to healing, not physically and not spiritually. To fight only causes both sides to lose; you reduce your chances for physical healing, and you deprive yourself of the chance for further inner growth. Acceptance, however, is always healing: it ensures that you do not exclude reality, but rather that you are present and therefore remain 'connected' to life. That creates the best environment possible for healing on all levels of your existence.

*

Don't think:
Oh, so acceptance is a guarantee for healing.

*

Maybe, at first, your physical reality will not change as quickly as you'd hoped and expected (and you can apply this to all sorts of crises: a divorce, illness or the death of a loved one, the loss of a job or going bankrupt). But when you take on the inner challenge hidden in the crisis, every unpleasant situation becomes a healing moment for your soul. If, after taking on this challenge, it turns out you also healed physically, it means a double healing took place for you: one in the outer world and one in the inner world. Think back to this paragraph the next time you are faced with a painful situation. What do you choose in that moment: do you bravely offer space to reality – no matter how frightening it is – or do you resist?

Creation or manipulation?
Acceptance is not wanting to change anything, but wanting what is, without the secret desire or hope that once you do this, a reward is waiting for you. Your reward is relaxing into your reality. Nothing more. The power of intention and of thought should therefore only be used for one goal: to offer space to

reality, in not to wanting to change the current reality. It should be a tool for co-creation, not manipulation.

*

Reality is already here, we don't have to create it.

*

To co-create means that you create with and from a sense of complete trust in the higher order. To force reality into what you want it to be is manipulation, because for some reason you are under the impression that you know better than the higher order does. So many books have been written, so many gurus are rising to the occasion, all of them trying to convince us that we can arrange and fix everything to get what we want on this earth by using the power of hope, religion, intention and thought. While the time has come for people to be reminded of their own, long-forgotten role in their own creation power, this type of New Age thinking is really just another attempt to lull humanity into a false sense of security.

If you really think about it, there is not a lot to create. As my friend and medium Percy Dens always says: Reality is already here, we don't have to create it; we only need to experience it so we can gain insight into how we divide instead of connect. Read this last sentence again. It really is an eye opener when it comes to creation, and a stark contrast to what you would expect when using the word 'creation'. But he is absolutely right, you cannot create a bigger reality, you can only experience a bigger reality by giving up your resistance against it.

*

*The most powerful factor in any
creation process is surrender.*

*

So therefore the most powerful factor in any creation process is surrender. The inability to surrender will prevent us from experiencing things fully, and that is caused by our fear of letting go. I have said it before: creation is, in fact, not a strained or difficult process by the mind but rather a relaxed and easy movement. You don't have to jump through all kinds of hoops to just be. You only need to let go, so you are free to jump, free to surrender to life. When it comes to co-creation and personal sustainability, most people forget one thing: you cannot mentally 'override' your soul's plan and the higher order. First of all, you have your 'conscious will' and your 'unconscious will', which are often not even congruent. On a conscious level you could desperately want something – curing your arthritis, for example – but on a subconscious level you may be blocking this healing because you are attached to the comfort zone being sick offers you.

*

Getting what you want is the result of transcending your neediness.

*

On a conscious level you may want to find the love of your life, but you may be blocking this on an unconscious level because you fear a real connection or you feel you don't deserve it. We can come up with all sorts of things by using our conscious will, but beneath the surface our unconscious will is co-creating constantly; and it is usually the one in charge, without us knowing. This is why some results taking place in reality can feel totally illogical to many people: 'Huh? But this isn't what I wished or visualized!' Or: 'Why don't I get all the things I focus on mentally?'

Summary:

1} Our conscience has an unbelievable influence on the chemistry of our body. The way you feel in your skin mirrors your consciousness.

2} Also important: what is your basic attitude towards the events in your life? All possible emotions only have two sources: love or fear. You could also say: trust or distrust. Love is relaxing for your body; fear is stressful for your body.

3} Every cell in your body is aware of what your brain is thinking, of your mood changes and of your deepest convictions.

4} Our body is ruled by our consciousness. If it changes, then the whole energy of your body will change. New science has shown us that it is even possible to change your genes this way.

5} Emotions and thoughts are powerful creation instruments, and we are constantly finding new ways on how you can consciously apply this power as a useful tool.

6} But don't think: I want to accept reality with all my being right now, because then I will quickly get what I want, then I will heal this condition I have or then I will live longer. Because that is not the way it works. Acceptance means to fully embrace what is, without reservation, without ifs and buts, without a goal, without any attachment to the result.

a dialogue
with life

A CONVERSATION WITH GREGG BRADEN

*If people knew that nothing can happen
unless the entire universe makes it happen,
they would achieve so much more
while using far less energy.*

– SRI NISARGADATTA

Trust the process
If you are a loyal reader of my books, you know what I think
about co-creation and about being the co-creator of your own
existence. Of course, I'm a firm believer in the magical power of
our thoughts and convictions; I've seen more than enough proof
of this in my own life. However, I've also learned that co-creating
your existence is something very different from, as I explained
in the previous chapter, simply overriding your current reality

with an insatiable 'me' mentality: I want, I want, I want! If I just tell myself something often enough, it will become the truth; if I imagine something hard enough, and think positive, the world around will change automatically.

*

The idea that we can simply impose our will onto the universe is false and misleading.

*

That's just not how it works. The universe is not the home-shopping network selling you instant and total happiness, inner peace and success. Because in order to create the life you want to lead, you should obviously first check and see with what tools you are creating it. Most people still create from their unconscious – from a place deep inside, a place they don't even know or want to know. A place, moreover, that is full of doubt, fear, resentment, negative thoughts, feelings of guilt and pain. You create, simultaneously, with your conscious and unconsciousness beliefs and convictions. The effect of your intentions is influenced by the extent to which these two are in agreement. This is because you may want something very much on a clear and conscious level, but, below the surface, your unconscious also continues to create what it wants with all its heart.

To recognize and dismantle your unconscious and its contradicting programming, the first step is learning to work with the universal laws of creation. The idea that we can impose our will onto the universe is false and misleading. No matter how much we all want that magical solution outside of ourselves, and hope that an easy *The Secret*-type of happiness exists, the reality is that there is no way to get around the development of self-knowledge.

Our intense focus on the self-conscious shaping of our existence is also a huge pitfall: while we're so busy trying to gain or keep control over everything, there is a distinct possibility that, meanwhile, life has something entirely different in mind for us, something that will bring us much closer to ourselves – and to real power and happiness – than all of those demands and wishes made by our inner 'I'. So it's important to leave our 'I' (with all its delusions of grandeur) at home, especially when we're working with the laws of creation; we must have trust in the process. We constantly receive a huge amount of clues showing us that we are all part of a much bigger plan than we could ever imagine.

Wu wei: the art of doing nothing

It's easy to miss those valuable clues if we don't watch out. The key to true happiness is found in trusting that everything happens for a reason when a specific wish doesn't come true; we should accept that whatever comes our way is part of life, and see it as a kind of medicine, as a logical part of what we've been brought here to do. If you can start to see things in this way and tune into the Greater Whole – and consciously walk the path that will help you become the person you were meant to be – then you will be given whatever tools you need to get there. Because in that moment, you are far more receptive and in tune with everything, instead of mentally pushing and pulling life in your direction.

*

To find peace is all about doing nothing
and letting life do the work for you.

*

Finding peace is all about doing nothing and letting life do the work for you. The less you do, the more you can allow things to come to fruition. That way, there isn't a constant busy signal on your telephone line with the universe, and you can allow life to have a chance to work for you. The Taoists call this the wu wei, which means something like the art of effortless action (not-doing), going with the flow, taking action without action, without using force.

However, Taoism is not a lazy philosophy by any means. It demands absolute clarity and attention, and for you to continually offer space to reality. It is about noticing your resistance, in every situation, so you can participate with your entire being in the natural flow of life. You don't need to do anything else. So it's not something you need to be proud of.

The Taoists call it purposeless wandering amidst the Tao. In Taoism, it is important to trust in the natural order of all things. Because in the non-action, the not-doing, things become clearer, and the truth, in any area, always comes to light.

Participation in creation

When I speak to Gregg Braden about personal sustainability and our constant need for control, he prefers to use the term 'anticipate' rather than 'creating'. The exceptionally charming and *The New York Times*-bestselling author of books like *The Spontaneous Healing of Belief, Fractal Time* and *The Divine Matrix*, says: "It has been my experience that what matters most is how we identify ourselves and what meaning we choose to give to the events that happen in our lives. So it's not about trying to control and influence events outside of you, but to ask yourself: 'What are my choices here and how can I best participate and respond to the reality of this moment?'"

*

It is about what meaning we choose
to give to what happens to us.

*

I ask Gregg: "Isn't that the exact opposite of what *The Secret* tells us, that we have the ability to change, shape and mould everything around us into what we want and that we are in control of our own happiness?" He answers diplomatically: "I know a lot of people who contributed to *The Secret*; I was also asked to contribute to it, but chose not to because it didn't come with the same charge as my message. Even though the book and the movie undoubtedly opened many doors to a new way of thinking and helped people figure out their roles in reality, sadly *The Secret* was interpreted by many in a very materialistic way. That was not the intention of the makers, but that is how it was used. Yet both the movie and the book were important because they encouraged us to look at the world from a new and different perspective." Gregg goes on to say: "I am a scientist. I was always taught that we are separate from the world outside of ourselves and that we have no influence on it. Well, after 30 years and many trips to all the corners of the world, I came in contact with a forgotten part of reality and with ancient and forgotten knowledge which has since taught me the exact opposite."

*

From our very first breath we speak a language without words: the language of the heart.

*

"The many different cultures, old civilizations and teachings that I came across during my stay in Bolivia, Egypt, India and Tibet show us that, from the moment we are born and take our first breath, we speak a language without words: the language of the heart. This language gives us the power and ability to heal ourselves, our body – and the world. This is very important, because when you understand this, you also understand that we – whether we're conscious of it or not – continually participate in the world we all share. This has nothing to do with controlling it, manipulating it or forcing our will onto reality, but we are simply participating in creation."

*

We have no control of what happens,
but we are in constant dialogue with life.

*

Not spectators but participants

"One of the most famous scientists of our time was the physicist John Wheeler. He was a colleague of Albert Einstein and was best known for his contribution on the development of the first atomic bomb, but also because he invented the names of two notable astronomical phenomena that became known as the Wormhole (1957) and the Black Hole (1967). He died quite recently in 2008 and came to the same conclusion. He said: "We live in a world that is not finished yet. We are all small parts of the overall plan of creation. Not spectators of the universe, as science once lead us to believe, but participants. Wheeler said it right: 'We must replace the word 'spectator' with the word 'participant'. We are in constant dialogue with life."

Heart coherence

"Today's science shows us that a continuous conversation takes place between our heart and our brain. This is also called 'coherency', and based on the idea that whatever we feel in our heart sends a signal to our brain, which influences the chemistry of our body and therefore the rest of the world around us."

*

The human heart is the most powerful generator of
electronically charged information in the body.

*

"Our heartbeat, brainwaves and breathing all have a certain rhythm. With a higher heart coherence, these rhythms begin to resonate, which then causes a certain kind of vibrational frequency in our brain, helping our heart and our body to communicate with each other optimally. You can see it as a beautiful sinus wave. This vibrational frequency has a positive effect on our own mind and body. When our brain receives high-quality signals from the heart, the brain will send out a high-quality signal to our body cells, and this also has a healing effect on the world outside of us."

The heart is stronger than the brain

"Our body and the world around us is composed of energy fields. These are inextricably linked with each other and influence each other incessantly. Some of these energy fields are electric, other magnetic, and quantum fields are part of it as well. Our world consists of electromagnetic and quantum energy fields. So it makes perfect sense that we use that energy to communicate; after all, we are not outside of it, but we are all a part of it."

*

The brain gets its information from the heart.

*

"What modern-day science has shown us over the past three or four years is that the human heart is the most powerful generator of electronically charged information in our body. Maybe even one hundred times more powerful than our brain. In the past, we were always told our brain was in charge. Everything happened there, and from there everything came into existence and motion. But modern-day science shows us that the brain receives its information from the heart and that the magnetic force (the attraction) of the heart is 5,000 times stronger than our brain. The only way to access that electro-magnetic power is by having a certain type of feeling. By accessing the right feeling, we access the power source and we can influence our body and the whole world around us deeply. So you create far more with who you are than by what you think."

Becoming what we want to experience outside ourselves
"This is really the core of all the old spiritual traditions. But we don't know the science behind it. Take the monks in Tibet, for instance, who live their lives very differently from us; because of that they have no attachment to modern-day science, but they hold the secret behind how you can create the feeling (vibrational frequency) with which you can change and heal your body and the world around you. So they knew long ago that by knowing with your heart, you can create a vibrational frequency which helps to create peace between tribes, peoples, leaders and countries. Again, not by wanting to manipulate, dominate or control, but by influencing it by simply being."

*

We should claim all things with our heart
instead of thinking about them with our brains.

*

"We must first become that which we want to experience outside of ourselves. We should claim all things directly with our heart instead of thinking about them first with our brains. This is a difficult task for Westerners. For instance, when I say to a Western audience: 'Follow your heart', they find this hard to do because they have been so conditioned to live and function only in their mind. So what do they do? They start to think about what it means to follow their heart ...

"So I teach them the old spiritual techniques to get them out of their heads and into their hearts. They are quite simple, by the way. For example, I ask them to touch the area of their heart with their finger tips or some part of their hand in the centre of their chest. The sensation of light pressure in the area of their heart causes their attention to focus there. This is one of the secrets of keeping the focus in your heart. This is why the monks do this for hours on end in the monasteries."

The architect of our experiences?
"People today often get stuck because they try to be the architect of their experiences and existence instead of living from their 'heart field' and allowing life to flow. By saying 'I want this to happen but not that' or 'This has to go this way or that way', many people put a lock on their lives and experience many problems. It is misleading to give people the feeling that they can change their lives and heal themselves through the power of intention and thought. This is also why so many people become frustrated, because, for them, applying *The Secret* doesn't seem to work."

*

The magnetic force of the heart is 5,000 times stronger than the brain.

*

"I don't believe that we have control over what happens to us. I think at best we can tip the scale in our favour a little bit. We're learning more about our relationship with the world we live in, and we are beginning to understand we are all a part of it. But – and for Westerners this is relatively new – what we do with this information depends on the maturity of the soul of the person in question. Someone who has only just come into contact with this information will test this knowledge and power based upon his or her values, like material wealth; but someone whose values are about the care of others, involvement, healing and peace will use this new knowledge in a positive way."

Don't think, but feel

"But why are so many people still so unhappy, while many of us have since learned that we play a much quieter role in life than we use to think?" I ask Gregg. He answers: "Because most people still function from the ego's urge to control the world, and they are not yet able to claim their existence from their heart. Only by letting go of the judgements about yourself and your body which come from your head can you become one with your body. According to the Taoists, this is a condition to becoming one with the world."

*

The more acceptance you have in your heart,
the more you contribute
to the peace in your body and the world around you.

*

"Someone who accepts who they are, who feels at home with him/herself and their body, is happier and more social than those who doesn't accept themselves. These people are more likely to look for happiness in outward appearances – for example, beautifying or improving the body – while inner healing is really what they need. From there you live in coherency and you claim the life that belongs to you. From this place of self-acceptance and inner peace you are like a 'small ink drop of acceptance' that changes the colour of the whole can of water. The more acceptance you have in your heart, the more you contribute to the peace in your body and the world around you. And when you have acceptance and love, you also attract acceptance and love. When you are peaceful, you attract peace. The magnetic force of your heart is unprecedented."

Life becomes the prayer

"An interesting scientific experiment was done during the

first Lebanese-Israeli war in the early eighties. The results were published in 1988 in *The Journal of Conflict Resolution*. Two hundred people were trained to feel peace in their heart. Not by thinking about it with their minds, but by really feeling it in their hearts. They then took these people to the Middle East, and at certain moments they were told to do what they were trained to do.* What did the scientists discover? That the moment these people felt peace in their heart, the building where they stayed (a hotel or conference room in a hotel) and the community around it were all deeply influenced. Terrorist activity stopped, fewer crimes were committed, and the amount of emergency-room visits in hospitals decreased as well as traffic accidents. As soon as these people stopped with their meditation, all of these things came back with a vengeance. They performed this experiment many times over and discovered that there is a very close connection between the feeling of peace in your heart and the influence of it on a broad geographical area."

*

They discovered that there is a close connection between
the feeling of peace in your heart
and the influence of it on a broad geographical area.

*

"Sceptics said: 'If the effect of this is so great, why does it stop when people stop their meditation?' That's exactly what this is all about! This is not something we do once in a while; it's a way of being and of life. Life becomes the prayer. It's not something where you say: 'OK, I am meditating at 12 o'clock to get into my heart and then I am done and I leave.' No, meditation is not – like so many people believe – meant as a spiritual little technique which you apply at a set time schedule (as a tool for the ego that still wants to remain in control). It is about learning to live life from that place within yourself."

Not working towards a result

"During my lectures I usually show the audience a movie made in a traditional Chinese hospital. In the movie you see three therapists who are trained to get into their heart coherence. You also see a woman with a tumour. On the ultrasound screen you can see how the tumour responds to their emotional state. The moment they get into their heart coherency, the tumour disappears from the screen. In three minutes. The obvious question is: what did the therapists feel? The answer is: they took their feeling from a place where the woman was already healed; they accepted the miracle of the cure as if it had already taken place. And please note: there is a very subtle difference between working towards a particular result (healing) and the quantum principle, which means you begin with the desired outcome. To start there and to already be what you want to experience and totally identify with it. You claim it by feeling it if it already took place and by being grateful as if it already happened."

So it is really about the absolute inner knowledge that whatever you have claimed already took place. There is no doubt. You accept that you are part of your world, that your heart has the ability to make a difference in your life and your body. This is an entirely different way of looking at the world than the view of wanting to dominate, control or manipulate your reality. Gregg says: "It is about opening yourself up to the possibility of completely surrendering yourself to healing, peace and the outcome."

A loving universe?

"If we learn the 'language of the field', we learn to communicate with our heart and participate in the creation of the energy field, which we are a part of and in which we participate creatively. Then we also have to be willing to accept what the field has to show us. This is not easy for most people, especially when it comes to the painful things in life. Take our body and illness, for example. There is a belief system which says that everything that happens with our body shows us something, that the body is a symbol for the desires of our soul and that it sometimes tries to get our attention through ailments or illness. I have worked with therapists who were able to get to the bottom of this in the blink of an eye with someone. I have witnessed healings in my own life in an hour simply by dismantling a conviction or undoing the programming that I wasn't even aware of. Many people resist this and do not want to hold themselves accountable for it. They say: 'How can you say I caused this illness myself? They aren't ready to accept their relationship with the universe.'"

"So, the key question is," I ask Gregg, "do you believe you are part of this universe or that you are separated from it? Do you think you are some coincidental creation or do you think you are here for a purpose?" He admits: "Yes, and you can add to that the questions: do you believe that the universe is loving and compassionate and wants only the best for you? Or do you believe the universe is not loving and not compassionate and doesn't want the best for you? Do you believe life is a safe place where a certain type of order prevails, even if sometimes we cannot see it? Or do you believe that life is a dangerous, insecure place, kept together by randomness?"

*

*Are you prepared to accept your relationship
with the universe?*

*

"I was raised on the idea that this is a very dangerous world and that you should always watch your back and look out for danger. And if something beautiful happens, or if you have something beautiful like a relationship, you should be careful that it is not taken away from you. If you're a child, you do not know any better than that, so this then is true. Fortunately, at some point that belief changed into my own belief because my actual experience in the world was very different. The key question is therefore: what kind of world do we claim for ourselves, in what kind of world do we believe? From there everything starts, from that belief everything comes into existence. Because if you, consciously or unconsciously, have the inner conviction that your world is frightening, then you will never be able to accept healing, your belief is that the world is against you, that life is an enemy who has wronged you."

To transcend suffering through acceptance

"We transcend suffering if we are in a state of acceptance. I spent a lot of time in monasteries in Tibet. The women are not well off there. There are also a lot of women in prison, under even worse circumstances. But when I look into their eyes, I see they are not angry or bitter, which is something they could easily be. I asked them why not, and the word they used was compassion. In Buddhism, this means that no matter what happens, you accept what happens as a part of a greater plan, which you may not understand at this moment. They do their very best, but also accept what cannot be changed until the day that it can be changed. Until then they can certainly choose to be bitter and angry, which they know is harmful to them and to their body and it shortens their own lives, or they can be healthy and choose the relaxation that acceptance brings them."

*

Acceptance doesn't change what happens,
but it changes our feeling about what happens.

*

"That brings us back to the beginning of our conversation: it is all about what meaning we give to things and the importance we ascribe to things. Look at holocaust survivors. Some didn't know how to handle their anger and bitterness and died soon after their release. Others, however, developed a form of acceptance and were able to continue life, despite all the pain. Acceptance doesn't change what happens, but it changes our feeling about what happens. That is what makes acceptance such a healing power."

stop working on yourself

*That's the only problem: the illusion about how you are
and how you should be
and the illusion that you cannot and should not
have certain facets and attitudes.*

– EVA PIERRAKOS

Who is working on what?
The whole concept of 'becoming what you are hoping to find
outside of yourself' that Gregg Braden speaks of is something
very different from the concept of 'working on yourself.'
Working on yourself as an action doesn't even exist. It is an
illusion. Because the question is: who's working on what?

*

The 'I' blocks you from being present.

*

Stop working on yourself

The answer is: the ego always wants to change reality because it always has something to complain and whine about. It has all sorts of preconceived notions and concepts about how life should be. It thinks it should be better because otherwise things will end badly for us. I often hear people say things such as 'I'm totally stuck and I can't seem to get ahead' or 'I can't seem to accept myself for who I am'. Precisely – your 'I' is unable to accept the real you as it is. The 'I' blocks you from being fully present.

The whole concept of working on yourself suggests that something needs to be fixed or improved upon, or that incredible changes must take place first before you can become happy. But this point of view will only bring you to a grinding halt. It is only aimed at maintaining an idea, a concept, a thought from the 'I' about who you should be, how your life should look, about everything that is wrong and what keeps you from finally being able to live your life fully.

So working on yourself is something that comes from a type of pinball-machine way of thinking; it's a term the 'I' came up with. Nothing is right, so we must do something about it. But there is nothing to 'do'. There is nothing to apply here. One of the greatest misconceptions that has come from the whole 'consciousness factory' is that we must first work really hard on ourselves before we can become happy. It all has to be different and better than it is now because the way you're doing it now is wrong. This way of thinking is what serves and fuels your 'I'.

The tricks of the 'I'

Nothing is imperfect. We are not lacking anything. Nothing we think we need is missing; otherwise, we would have it. These types of thoughts are the kind of tricks the 'I' plays on us so that we continue to search, strive and work. But every time you go into search mode, you actually create more of a void because you think something in your life or a situation is missing. Why? Because the ego is present during your search-and-strive mission. But if and when you decide to go and be happy in the here and now, then it loses its purpose and all of its power. As long as you do not realize this, you are offering it room to keep convincing yourself that your life is still not perfect or complete, and it will continue to attract a demand in your life. After all, it must continue to secure its existence.

*

Living spiritually is not the same as controlling and managing all your thoughts and feelings.

*

Because so many people's basic beliefs come from this feeling of something missing, they spend a lot of time and energy fighting experiences that they don't want or changing the things about themselves or others that they don't like. But what is important is that we actually stop all the 'doing'. It's not about improving yourself. Living spiritually is not the same as controlling and managing all your thoughts and feelings. It is not about fighting against all your patterns and convictions. It is not about changing how you are now but about relaxing into who you are now. It is only about one thing: to offer space to reality without resistance. This will allow more of a release and relaxation to enter your life, and your life energy can start to flow again. Problems will evaporate into thin air because whatever you no longer judge loses its power.

*

Nothing we think we need is missing; otherwise, we would have it.

*

You'll notice that your mind will become more energized and clear. Your relationships will become easier. You will find yourself experiencing more seemingly coincidental events and meetings. This is because you have moved yourself to a completely different vibrational frequency by consciously stepping out of your resistance. By accepting what is, you take away what is blocking you and your energy can flow freely again. When you stop wanting to control and manage everything that happens, you will find that things work out on their own.

Acceptance in the real world

How do you do all of that? Very easy: by doing it. No matter how scary it feels at first. Imagine the following: something happens, or you feel something. Normally, you would back away, but this time you stay in the thought, or literally in the situation, where you are. Feel the resistance, feel your body protest, but continue to take deep and relaxed breaths. Don't move an inch, don't step aside, but remain completely present in the situation or in the feeling that you experience as unpleasant or painful. There you go! That is giving up your resistance, now you've taken the 'I' out of the equation. That is surrendering to the shapeless world of the now. That is acceptance.

You cannot practise surrender and acceptance – you just have to do it. It's also not something you use to get rid of a particular feeling, or to make reality more bearable or to achieve some other goal. Acceptance is, once again, nothing more than no longer resisting. So give as much space as possible to reality, your thoughts and feelings.

*

*Spread your arms wide and be free of judgement –
for yourself and for others.*

*

Dutch TV-maker and author Annemiek Schrijver wrote a practical and beautiful interview about surrender: "A few weeks ago I went out to dinner with an old friend who said to me with a very serious face: 'I did not like your last book!' Five years ago I would have completely shut down. Now I think: he is welcome to have that opinion. Because of my attitude, the dinner remained pleasant and intimate. What I felt was: let me embrace you, you are welcome with or without your venom. This is my latest insight: others are not only welcome with their softer side but also with their pain and venom. That way, you spread your arms wide and free yourself of judgement – for yourself and for others."

Resistance against the resistance
Warning for the perfectionists among us: don't see it as a problem when you don't succeed in this right away, when you become angry or sad when you find yourself in this type of situation, and when you still feel resistance or by allowing certain feelings in. Be cautious of your resistance against the resistance. Everything is merely an experience. There is no right or wrong. Try to remain neutral and therefore free of judgement – also against yourself.

*

*Accepting things as they are instantly gives you
a feeling of great power and healing.*

*

See, feel and taste life as it is – observe yourself as you are. Stay with it, keep your attention on what is, also when it becomes difficult or painful. You will find it is not as threatening or destructive as it seems. Accepting things as they are and daring to feel them as they are instantly gives you a feeling of great power and healing. The moment you give up your urge to want to control and fully step into reality, you will experience life in a fundamentally different way.

What is your shadow side?

To face yourself and your life completely, and accept who and where you are now, leads to real clarity and to transformation. This is the only type of work you can do on yourself. Self-examination is nothing more and nothing less than when you experience turmoil to look at what happens without any judgement. Do you experience stress? Are there problems? Then take your time and see what the 'I' story is that you have created and have started to believe about yourself. Most of the time, we are the slaves of our own subconscious programming, conditioning and convictions. It is usually the very restrictive and limiting programming, conditioning and convictions dictating to us how we should behave to feel safe and loved.

*

*Most of the time we are the slaves
of our own subconscious programming.*

*

They are also called 'pictures', and they usually begin during our early childhood. No matter how good our childhood was, we are all raised with the truths of others. We are all dealing with the emotional and spiritual heritage of our parents and/or grandparents. During our childhood we all experience things through our upbringing and education that unconsciously give us messages like: you are not good enough (yet) as you are. A lot still needs to happen before you matter, before you can claim your birthright. It's got to be better. You have to become something when you grow up. Your true self is not good enough yet or isn't even welcome.

*

Self-examination is nothing more and nothing less than when you experience moments of turmoil and look at what happens without any judgement.

*

So, some important questions are: as an adult, how good are you at expressing your emotions, feelings and thoughts? Are you unafraid to show yourself as you really are? Or do you suppress a big part of who you really are? In short: what you don't show, the parts of yourself you don't allow to be, whatever is avoided, suppressed or needs to be hidden, that is your shadow side. It could very well be that you are totally unaware of these 'pictures'. This makes it difficult for you to recognize them. In that case I say: take a look at your life. Is there turmoil? Stress? A sense of lack or loss? Are there reoccurring problems in your relationships? Then those are all manifestations of your shadow side.

You are not your thoughts
Observe your life and look closer at what stories you've started to believe about yourself. Maybe you've started thinking you're not quite there, that it all has to be better before you can relax into the reality of now. For a long time I also believed this story. It could always be better, because who and where I was was never enough. This was not really my own thought, but one that came from my own family legacy. This kind of legacy is a lot like a flea. It jumps from generation to generation, from family to family, from family member to family member. This continues until someone in that long line sees what is really going on. If this doesn't happen, then this type of programming will continue to overshadow many lives. As long as we don't examine these convictions, we remain slaves to them and continue down this path like a hamster running in a spinning wheel.

*

You are not your story
but the light that shines through that story.

*

And that's a shame, because they are just thoughts. Yet those unconscious thoughts can determine your whole life without you even noticing it. Take a look at the thoughts that occur to you which give you so much turmoil and grief. Try to imagine how you would feel if those thoughts did not occur in your consciousness.

Who and where would you be?

Is working on yourself nothing more than recognizing this? The answer is: yes, it really is nothing more than that. You free yourself from the grip your thoughts have on you when you completely let go the thoughts that are painful inside, and then test their level of truth. You free yourself the moment that you and consciousness are merely witnesses to all those passing thoughts, and accept that this stream of thoughts is not you.

Summary

1} 'Working on yourself' is an expression that comes from the pinball machine that is your mind.

2} In order to create space, allow yourself to be fully present; concepts like imperfection, lack or loss are totally useless. Nothing is imperfect, we are not lacking anything, and nothing we need now is missing; otherwise, it would already be here.

3} It's not about changing how you are now, but about relaxing into who you are now.

4} To face yourself and your life completely, and accept who and where you are now, leads to real clarity and to transformation. This is the only type of work you can do on yourself. Self-examination is nothing more or nothing less than looking at what happens without any judgement during moments of turmoil.

5} Do you experience stress? Are there problems? Then take your time and see what 'I' story you have started to believe about yourself.

6} By accepting what is, you take away what is blocking you and your energy can flow freely again. More ease and relaxation will come into your life and problems will seem to evaporate, since, if you have no judgement on something, it loses its power.

what you
resist persists

When you surrender and stop resisting and stop trying to change that which you cannot change, but be in the moment, be fully open to the blessings you've already received and those that are yet to come [...] the literal vibration of your life will change.

– OPRAH WINFREY

Petting the monster

Happiness and fulfilment certainly exist, and our desire to achieve them is understandable and natural. But it is not some sort of reward for good behaviour given to you by something outside of yourself for something you did. It is simply the result of relaxing into the reality of the moment, having the courage and honesty to look at how you are right now and especially at those parts of yourself you would rather avoid altogether. The key is to tolerate everything in and about yourself, whether it's pain, suffering, fear, cruelty, malice or jealousy. Everything is a part of you, so why would you want to get rid of a part of yourself? Why would you make something inside of you into an enemy that you have to fight?

*

Why would you make something inside of you into an enemy?

*

When you look at most of the successful treatment methods for addictions, for example, none of the methods are based on a struggle. Struggling against what is will only lead to the problem becoming bigger. In order to bring people with compulsions closer to a feeling of ease and happiness, the only meaningful thing to do is to reconcile with what is, no matter how ugly that reality may appear to be when you look at it with your personal conscience and all its judgements. Telling people that a specific part of them is undesirable is the same as rejecting the whole person. Besides, most people prone to addiction (usually very intelligent, sensitive people) are very familiar with rejection through self-criticism, so that won't help them at all.

*

When you truly connect to something, get a real feel for it, you will see its true nature.

*

What does help most people who are struggling with an addiction, whether it's an eating, drinking, sex, bungee-jumping or negative-thinking addiction, is the total acceptance of what is. It is important to encourage those with an addiction not to reject things about themselves, but to actually allow everything in – even the most destructive patterns. The biggest monster turns into a meek little lamb when you pet it and ask: so tell me, what is it you're doing here and what do you need?

But if you chain it down in a dark dungeon, without giving it love and attention, it becomes a wild animal which will eventually become unstoppable. What you suppress or hide, don't acknowledge or do not recognize, becomes even stronger. The more you wish to compensate for something about yourself or to convince others of something, the stronger your shadow side will eventually manifest itself.

*

*Acceptance and surrender are about letting go
of illusions and wrong assumptions.*

*

In the book *Anger, Buddhist Wisdom for Cooling the Flames*, the Vietnamese Buddhist monk and Zen master Thich Nhat Hanh shows us that it doesn't pay to suppress, fight or deny negative emotions. Anger, for example, is one of the most powerful negative emotions a human being can have. But in order to experience happiness, it is of great importance that this destructive, negative energy is transformed into positive energy. However, the transformation of anger, or any kind of negative aspect, can only take place when you acknowledge everything as a part of yourself.

He says: "Embrace your anger and give it your sincere and genuine attention. Genuine attention helps us to become conscious of what is really going on. Genuine attention is touching, recognizing, acknowledging, greeting, embracing … When you truly come in contact with something and get a real feel for it, you will see its true nature. Which will lead you to insight and, with that, you can transform the energy into something positive."

To return to your life's joy and life's energy, it is important to unleash all aspects of yourself that you think shouldn't or cannot be there. After all, you are a whole human being. Your 'I' can govern your thoughts and say: this part of you is allowed, but this part is not. Maintaining that story is a constant weight on your psyche, and it undermines your life energy and your emotional, physical and spiritual vitality.

The fact remains that you are both and all parts. You aren't half of yourself but always whole. Acceptance and surrender are about letting go of any and all illusions and (wrong) assumptions. Because your wholeness cannot disappear. It is what you've always been, and always will be. It's your true nature. So you don't become whole by being perfect, but by allowing yourself to be a complete human being.

A note for coaches

If you are a coach, the following is very important: the work your clients need to carry out should be aimed at letting them become who they are instead of who they want to be or think they should be.

Learning to tolerate everything in and about yourself

Learning to tolerate everything in and about yourself is the essence of learning to tolerate our earthly life and also, therefore, the beautiful things. Does this sound strange? Maybe so. But take a closer look at yourself and all around you: the saddest part is that, despite all our wishes and desires, we are often not even able to tolerate real happiness and real love, as most of us aren't free on the inside yet and haven't reconciled with ourselves. Thus there is literally no inner space for us to experience any real happiness. Unconsciously, a little voice tells us, 'You are not allowed to enjoy and relax. You don't deserve it yet because you're not there yet, you still have a suspicious amount of faulty human traits, so I won't give you what you want.'

*

You don't become whole by being perfect,
but by allowing yourself to be a complete human being.

*

We put a lot of conditions on our lives. Only when I'm more in balance, more patient and thinner, or more energetic or accomplished, do I deserve love. Just look at how often people reject happiness (unconsciously) when it comes their way. People tend to back or push away (unconsciously) exactly the things they want most in their life. The culprit here is that unconscious little voice. That unconscious little tyrant is whispering to us from the sidelines, 'What if it all goes wrong?' You fail, lose it again and experience pain, or cannot realize or accomplish something.

Most of the time it is about taking responsibility for the fact that it is your own desires from which you are running away. Usually, you do this in such a subtle way that later you say to yourself, 'You see, it didn't work out again, I am better off alone.' Or: 'I wasn't meant for happiness and success.' Meanwhile, you don't even notice that, unconsciously, literally everything in you was aimed at confirming and realizing all of your preconceived ideas.

*

There is no one outside of yourself who will bring
you freedom.

*

To free your true creation power and life power, you will need to make contact with the negative, self-sabotaging side of yourself. Don't fight it, welcome it. Don't condone it, but have an honest look at it. You can only put changes into motion after you find out in which way you say 'no' to that which you desire most. If you aren't ready to take on this type of self-examination, then this book is not for you. Because there really is no way around it.

The guru in you

Only you can do it. There is no one outside of yourself who will bring you freedom or who holds the key to your happiness. There is no magic solution outside of yourself. The only solution is to become hyper-aware of what your unconscious motivation is. The only really meaningful question to ask here is: what really keeps me from doing something pleasant, something to ensure that I am satisfied with my life? To find out, it is essential that you learn to have a closer examination of your inner convictions, feelings and thought patterns.

Difficult? Yes! Mostly because those inner convictions, the ones that cause most of the misery, happen unconsciously. Therefore you cannot work on them directly, even if you wanted to. It's just up to you to become aware of them. But this is the beginning of an interesting and exciting journey. Because as soon as you involve the unconscious with your current reality, you will start to see the cause-and-effect connections. As soon as you involve your outside world with your inner world, you will start to look deeper into and recognize the meaning behind the appearance of everything that you find on your life's path and, in turn, the cause of your pain and feelings of loss.

*

You will become more conscious when you start to see what the cause is and what the effect is.

*

You will start to see that everything you experience as painful and annoying is the cause of your (unconscious) inner contradictions. And that a conflict outside of yourself always points to a conflict inside. There is inner resistance somewhere,

where something doesn't flow. So you become more conscious when you begin to see what the cause is and what the effect is. There is no development without taking on the personal confrontation with yourself. You don't need anything or anyone to do this – no workshops, coaching sessions, rites or ceremonies, spiritual illusionists, ego-tourists or someone who strokes your ego. You only need one true and honest guru and that is you.

Summary

1} The only way to regain joy and vitality in your life is to relax into the reality of the current moment and by embracing the aspects of yourself that you think shouldn't or cannot be there.

2} After all, you are a whole human being. Your 'I' can govern your thoughts and say, 'This part of you is allowed to be here and this part isn't.' But you aren't half of yourself, you are whole.

3} That wholeness cannot disappear. It is what you've always been and what you always will be. It's your true nature. You don't become whole by becoming perfect, but by allowing yourself to be a whole human being.

reconnecting with the cosmic frequencies

A CONVERSATION WITH DR ERIC PEARL

*In essence, healing is the following: releasing or removing
an obstacle that has kept us separated
from the perfection of the universe.*

– DR ERIC PEARL

Dr Eric Pearl and reconnective healing
The premise that our wholeness cannot disappear is also shared
by Dr Eric Pearl. It is his vision that we are not here to become
holy, but to become human. What a relief! During my life, I have
rarely come across people whose view on healing wasn't that

something is wrong and needs to be fixed as soon as possible, but rather that everything is as it should be, and for a good reason. Certainly not the people who are in the 'healing business'.

Reconnecting with the cosmic frequencies

The word 'healer' in itself already implies that something needs to be healed or fixed, and I am not so fond of that concept. First of all, it suggests that there is someone who can heal someone else (which is already a lie), and second, that someone needs to be healed (another lie). Moreover, it creates a hierarchical relationship (doctor-healer/patient) which I also don't believe in. You are always the healer and patient simultaneously. I call this the Taoist care model.

*

Every human being is the teacher and the student at the same time.

*

By this I mean that no one is only a teacher or a student, but that every person is a teacher and student at the same time. Doctor and patient, carer and those in need, those with the knowledge and those in need of knowledge. They are paternalistic dividing lines that don't really exist in reality, and they belong to the old world-view. When that insight and that modesty are not present, then there is no pure foundation for healing. Real healing can only take place when there is a real respect for the higher order of things. What happens is what can and should happen and not necessarily what we want to happen. Healings happen in everyone's life, only not always exactly in the manner that we think they should.

Eric Pearl expresses this surprisingly well. As he enters the stage in a packed hall in Amsterdam, I think to myself, 'What a strange man.' My whole body fills with resistance, and for a moment I think, 'I'm going home; I am not in the mood for this.' At that moment, I'm wasn't even sure why. Was it his looks, his exaggerated manners, his vanity and layers of makeup? I have no idea what it was, and yet he grabbed my attention. I had to keep watching and listening. What was this almost alien-like phenomenon I saw before me? I put my thoughts in neutral and surrendered to the event and also to the days following, in which my husband Robin and I took the reconnective healing seminar. I marvelled at the hundreds of volunteers he'd mobilized, from God only knows how many countries. How did he do that? Hey, I wanted that, too! So I put aside the judgement and distrust I had in self-proclaimed and overpaid gurus and quickly discovered one thing: Eric Pearl is really something else.

He is a real spiritual pain in the neck and I kind of like that. He tears apart all the well-known relations and structures and, as a healer, cleans it all back up by creating a prominent space for the higher order. Pearl is not a healer who sees health from the point of view that, if it is sick, it has to be made better, or if you're sick, then something is wrong.

*

Healing is something that the patient and the universe agree upon together.

*

He also tears apart the healer-patient relationship. He says: "In order to make it clear, I call myself a healer sometimes. But I don't heal anyone. Nobody heals anybody else. Your job as a healer is simply to 'listen' (with this I mean to be in a receptive state) and to remain open for the energy that makes you the catalyst for healing your patient." In his book he writes: "Healing is something that the patient and the universe agree upon together. The healing energy comes from the source and flows in and through us, from us and to us. This energy is like light that flows through a prism. We are the prism. We become one with the patient and the universe in generating a mutual energy field made from love (in the highest sense of the word) and a state of oneness. It's not like God chose you or me as a healer. That type of thinking is spiritual arrogance. It is certainly possible that we are a part of the healing process of someone else, but at the same time we must realize that the other also becomes part of our system."

Making space for healing
"For any type of healing to take place, we have to let go of disempowering questions like how and why," says Pearl. "We have to move beyond the boundaries we know. We have so many preconceived notions about what health is, or should be, that often we have no idea what to do with what our body does, or doesn't do, in reality. When our body doesn't do what we want or expect, it has to get better as soon as possible. But better than what?" says Pearl. "What does getting better really mean? Better than it was at some point before? Better than someone else? Becoming better is a very limited definition of healing."

*

*For healing we have to step out from
the boundaries we know.*

*

"Of course, healing can, as we often think, relieve symptoms. But healing also means that people become spiritually whole again. Who says that something goes wrong when you become ill or have a disability? Maybe this particular body is precisely the body you need for your inner growth at the moment. Or maybe an important message, lesson or experience for your surroundings is hidden in your illness or disability. Maybe there is a lot more going on than you can see with the naked eye."

Connected living

Clinician Eric Pearl discovered that the key to health and healing is something he calls the reconnection: a reconnecting with the energy lines that connect us to our body, with the energy fields around us, with the ley lines of our planet and from there with the energy grid of the whole universe. It brings us back in contact with the deeper connection to life. From this oneness comes healing. Real healing. Evolutionary healing.

*

Reconnective healing is healing through the transference of energy, light and information.

*

"Reconnective healing comes from a completely different point of view to the conventional view on health, and is not to be compared to energy healing," Pearl says repeatedly. "Reconnective healing is healing through the transference of energy, light and information." When we sit down in his dressing room after his performance, surrounded by makeup (a very funny detail to me is that he travels with a personal makeup artist), he says: "Everyone in the world can feel that the world we live in is changing profoundly. The earth is changing, the weather is changing, political and economic systems are changing, relationships change, you and I have changed, and our view on what health and happiness is has changed. Everyone, no matter where they are in the world or what economic-social class they are, is experiencing an enormous shift in consciousness. Everything, and I mean everything, is beginning to vibrate in a different rhythm and according to new laws. So we are all in need of new tools, convictions, new answers to the questions on how we live, to heal and to blossom; the answers and solutions from the old way of thinking and belief system simply won't do anymore."

*

*Everything is beginning to vibrate in a different rhythm
and according to new laws.*

*

"What we need, now more than ever," says Pearl, "is to reconnect to the original feeling of the connection to ourselves, the universe, nature and to all of life. That connection creates unity and order, and that order is healing. But humanity was separated from that kind of oneness in consciousness long ago. Once upon a time, our race was far better connected and more whole than we are now. There are many theories about how this division came to be. One thing is for sure: long before us, civilizations did manage to live connected to the cosmic frequencies. Every culture in history, from pre-biblical civilizations to the ancient Greeks, was familiar with an ancient, perfect world, without war or disease."

Although we were separated from the source at one point, the ability to collectively increase our consciousness to a level where we can take on and anchor these type of frequencies, has always been present inside of us. But we couldn't make the connection. Pearl says: "We have finally reached that level. That's why there are so many shifts taking place. New frequencies are available to us. These frequencies provide us with real power and strength from a place of purity and authenticity. Untruths and lies do not hold up in this frequency; contradictions and divisions disappear. We are in the middle of a heavy process of increasing our frequency that everyone deserves and concerns everyone. Nobody is excluded from this process, and everyone has the capability to come into contact with it. It is simply a gift that comes with this time period."

Plugging in

When I peeked into the various rooms during our three-day course, I saw aspiring Reconnection therapists, feverishly busy with connecting the people on their treatment tables to these new frequencies. I wasn't so sure this was the way to do it, because the way I saw it, most of these students were simply out to get their diploma as quickly as possible so they could start their own practice.

*

Connection ensures coherence and order,
and that order is healing.

*

One thing I do know: everything humanity is going through at the moment is one big invitation and opportunity designed to help us reconnect to the forgotten and lost frequencies that Pearl speaks of – a reconnection to our own soul nature, to the universe, to God. This connection also causes an instant shift: untruths and impurity must now make room for authenticity. Just look at your own life: the moment you are closer to yourself, faithful to yourself, live from your own strength and not from a place of neediness, the truth about so many things, which up until now you had kept in place artificially (coming from your need for a false sense of security and false acceptance), now come to light. This is how it works universally and globally. Connected living returns us to the truth of our true power, on all levels. To be disconnected, to me, simply means you are unplugged and that you are running around aimlessly on your own accord, outside of the giant cosmic web of primal powers; primal powers to which you have complete access but you cannot seem to reach or of which you cannot make use.

Energy, light and information

What has also become clear to me is that Pearl is a very brave physician and an amazing innovator. He is someone who, from his own conventional background and from a deeper knowing, left the beaten path with all the risks and consequences that come with doing so. Innovators don't usually have an easy time of it. Nevertheless, Pearl, with all his controversial views on healing, is being noticed by the more traditional medical world. He is often invited as a healer by hospitals and universities, and is widely supported and applauded by many new scientists.

*

To make room for healing, you must give up your attachment to the outcome.

*

This has to do with all the shifts taking place in our consciousness as well. Many health care professionals experience that, despite all the technical knowledge and advancement available to us, there are still many unanswered questions and problems that cannot be resolved without taking a broader view. More people are starting to think outside of the box, daring to go beyond their comfort zones, realizing there has to be more and are prepared to open themselves up and search for it.

More than anything, I see Pearl as a teacher in informative medicine, the medicine of the future. No more pills and powders, but working with light, energy and information, or frequencies. We're discovering that everything – every organ in our body – contains energy, light and information. This can all be measured and are all connected to the original, vital vibrational level. Even an aspirin has a vibrational frequency. Once you know how to capture it, at a certain point all you have to do is to take on its frequency. Thankfully, it is already taking place – for example, think about the Vitascanning I spoke of before; it is absolutely the way we will practise medicine in the future.

Who or what heals here?
Reconnective healing restores your connection to the cosmic

frequencies. Pearl is certain that this has an effect. But whether healing takes place on a physical, emotional or spiritual level is not up to us. What happens to you is not what you want or think you need, but what is necessary for the growth of your conscious.

*

So what is it that needs to be 'healed' with Annemarie?

*

Is healing physical by definition? No, Pearl is also very clear in this. During the third day of the course, a woman bolts to the microphone and asks, seemingly a little irritated: "I see that Annemarie Postma has been here for two days. Why don't you give her a healing?" I have found that Pearl is at his best during such unexpected moments. He answers: "What exactly needs to be healed in Annemarie?"

I know, it seems like a paradox: that a hall filled with 2,000 students who all want to become a 'reconnection practitioner' with healing as their goal are told that someone like me, with a disability, doesn't need to be healed. A bit confusing, I think. Yet, I didn't see anyone frown or scratch their heads, but I couldn't imagine that out of the 1,999 other people, no one had any questions about this because, to put it mildly, this is not exactly easy material. But OK, Pearl didn't seem to be bothered, so I decided not to be bothered either.

*

Not healing the illness or ailment but the person.

*

In any case, I found his answer to be fitting to my situation and how I experience it. His remark is precisely the reason why I found it so incredibly important to include his point of view in this particular book. "Not healing the illness or

137

ailment but the person," says Pearl. "What happens is what is needed to accomplish that. To accept that that is the road to true healing."

Abracadabra

"What a bunch of abracadabra," someone said after I had sent a few tweets on the subject onto the digital highway stratosphere. "Everybody just wants to be healed! Period." You see, that is exactly where the core of the problem lies. It is what most of us continue to resist. Most people simply don't want to believe that you don't just get what you think you need in life, or what you want to happen, but that what happens is precisely what is needed for your soul's evolution. But your personal conscious and ego cannot, and don't want to, understand or accept this. They simply believe they have a right to get what they are owed or what's coming to them.

*

Everyone heals, but not always in the way you expect.

*

"You know," Pearl says, "I have seen miraculous things happen by bringing people into contact with these frequencies. However, there are also healing treatments that do not bring the expected results. This can be because of several reasons. I have, meanwhile, learned that the problem is not that the person doesn't heal in the way you or they expected, but that the problem lies in the expectation itself. In the past, I used to say that everyone can heal. But I changed my mind. I still believe that everyone can heal, but not always in the way you expect them to heal. By acknowledging that healing means that you are reconnecting with the perfection of the universe, you also have to realize that the universe knows what you need to receive. The needs of the patient are recognized by the universe, which then creates the circumstances for the proper reaction to those needs. So, as a healer, it is important to take a step back and not direct or try to shape its meaning. To create space for a true healing, you have to give up your attachment to the outcome completely."

the tragedy
of the
endless search

It is only through searching, seeking,
desiring, that the ego exists.

– OSHO

Fire yourself as the critic of the now
What I found to be incredibly witty and engaging about Eric
Pearl was his ability to point out the painful truth regarding all
of the new age nonsense, and how he makes it clear that a lot
of what happens in the name of 'spirituality' is often nothing
more than exercises of the ego. Because of that, we keep going
around in the same circles. A while later I heard the following
funny story which was a perfect example of this theory. It
was about the founder of a well-known publishing house. A

real spiritual thinker and pioneer in his field. A man who had published and read thousands of books about spirituality. He had met hundreds of authors, gurus and coaches, attended and organized countless seminars, symposiums and workshops, elaborated on every conceivable piece on self-development and even published some things himself.

*

The search is a system that preserves and maintains itself.

*

These days, he is well beyond the age of retirement. A mutual acquaintance told me that our old friend had attended a workshop and afterwards told the acquaintance excitedly about the startling new insight he had gained from it. What was this incredible new insight? It is important ... to live from your heart.

Aha ... Our mutual acquaintance paused for a moment and carefully said: "Uh ... right. But haven't you heard this a million times before, during your 45-year career in the spirituality business?" Apparently not. This story illustrates perfectly what a tragedy the endless search is and, at the same time, how it is an addiction to what we believe is missing in our lives. The search is a system that always preserves and maintains itself. Over and over again, the searcher takes on a new truth in the hope that this new truth will finally end the search. If it's not a new truth, then just dress up an old one as new. As long as you continue your search, you believe that you need to find something that is better and more complete than this very moment. That way, you keep repairing and working on your landing gear so you will never actually have to make and experience the real landing.

The eternal paradox of the search

The real paradox about the search is that as long as you are searching, you are actually making it impossible for yourself to find something, because you are probably only focused on whatever it is that you are looking for. You are only aiming to find what you think you need to find, and in the meantime you could be missing all the things taking place right before your very own eyes. Searching will only lead to more searching. Truly finding something is only possible in complete freedom. That kind of freedom only comes when you fire yourself as the constant critic or reviewer of all that happens in the reality of the here and now. The search will end when you let go of all your opinions and resistance. You will find liberty when you no longer believe something is missing. The biggest changes will take place when you no longer believe something needs to be changed.

*

Your endless search is nothing more than
the utter avoidance of this moment.

*

It all sounds fairly simple, but apparently it's not. How many people do you know (I for one know many) who travel from seminar to seminar, course to course, devour book after book, take on inspiration after inspiration and one new insight after the other, without any of it ever creating a real change in their lives, without ever turning over the proverbial new leaf? I think many of us have come across these people, or maybe it even applies to you. The search in itself does have a function, but that function is – after a very long detour – really no more than finding out there really was nothing to find. We usually discover that all that searching and doing, through whatever spiritual traditions, rules, methods, codes and laws, was not really 'it' either. In that respect, your search does have some real value. Not because you will find what you're looking for, but because you start to see that it will not bring you what you expected.

Useful detours

This is not a book that is necessarily against the search. But if you feel you are a searcher, don't see it as a problem – you are doing nothing wrong. On the contrary. Often, we first have to travel the road in order to find out that, actually, we never had to leave where we were in the first place, and that we were already there to begin with. I am not implying that it is not useful to take the detour. I just want to make clear that the endless search at its core is always about the avoidance of the here and now and is thus an eternal confirmation that you are still not there.

There simply is no future where it will all be better. Inner peace, enlightenment and total freedom can only take place right now, in this very moment. As long as you think that you cannot be there yet, you are fooling yourself and going around in circles. The moment you realize this, the urge to search will disappear instantly.

*

As long as you think that you cannot be there yet,
you are just fooling yourself.

*

Have you ever read the story *Siddhartha* by Herman Hesse? No? Well, maybe you should take a break from this book and pick it up again after you've read this beautiful story. It is a striking way to illustrate that, no matter how long your spiritual journey takes and where it may lead, it will always bring you back to this moment. You can also read my book *The Secret Within – The Power of No Nonsense Spirituality*. I devoted a whole section in Chapter 6 to this wonderful tale written by Hesse.

In my opinion, there is no other story that so clearly shows us that all this 'spiritual searching' is, in fact, nothing more than a really long detour to the now. It's a real waste of time. A delay, postponement, more of the same. Maybe temporarily enlightening but never permanently satisfying or liberating. Why not? Because whilst you are working so hard on yourself and constantly searching, you're still stuck in the concept, a theory; a representation of how your imagination thinks things should be. No matter how spiritual and sublime it may appear to be, it will always continue to be a lot of mental pushing and pulling.

Letting go of definitions

The reason I wanted to write this book is so we can all finally say goodbye to these concepts and theories. I wanted to show how your thinking has a tendency to return to those definitions and ideas due to our constant need for security and assistance; to let you feel how your ego is always searching for comfort and guidance.

*

The spiritual industry only breeds more searchers.

*

The more you observe this type of thinking, the more you will recognize how much it is aimed at a life in some distant, imaginary future, where you will finally be satisfied with yourself and experience real peace and happiness. By doing that, your attention is not free to experience the current moment. You're always preoccupied with fixing the moment or working on something in your future. But where are you right now? The whole spiritual 'industry' is based on that concept. It is an industry that feeds on this manic way of thinking, and encourages and maintains the endless cycle of the search. So many spiritual magazines, newspapers, books, DVDs and TV shows promise us that somewhere, within ourselves or in life, there is a place where we can go, where it is more peaceful, safe, pleasant, quiet and sublime. This industry only breeds and creates more searchers because it maintains the whole endless search movement that is out there.

*

The ego gets absolutely no satisfaction
in accepting the here and now.

*

The difficult thing about the endless search is that we don't see that we are still starting out from the ego's perspective. Just think about it: we want to improve something about ourselves and about our lives. We want to be rid of something or want something that isn't there yet. We want to feel more 'whole' and 'complete'. We want change and development.

*

The difficult thing about the endless search is
that we still start from the ego's perspective.

*

The ego gets absolutely no satisfaction in accepting the here and now; it's way too busy always looking ahead, at the future, the next moment, the moment after and the moment after that. Once, one day soon, when I have reached it, I will find peace and happiness. I will find that partner who does see me for who I really am, I will earn more money, I will achieve all that success, status and recognition, I will finally have that beautiful beachfront home with the perfect sunset. But, of course, that day never comes. The ego's mantra continually feeds the endless search. Those who search will continue to search; those who strive will keep striving. That is because their quest, their endless search, is being driven by the resistance against what is.

The spiritual ego

Certainly, when we find ourselves on the spiritual path, this opposition, or resistance, can manifest itself in more sophisticated and subtle ways. The resistance is the same for everyone, but someone who is on a spiritual path can create excuses and interesting ways to describe it and manage to spin, rationalize and condone the truth.

*

The further away the goal or target, the bigger the ego.

*

The ego means not being present in the here and now, mentally being somewhere other than where your body is, searching and striving for a goal in the distant future. The goal of most truly spiritual people isn't that new job or a bigger house; it all goes way beyond that, even beyond all earthly things: salvation, enlightenment, God, immortality. A beautiful line by Krishnamurti: 'Whatever you do to be free from the self is also a self-centred activity.' These spiritual goals require us, therefore, to remain cautious, extra vigilant and alert. This is because often what we do in the name of 'spirituality' is nothing more than a mutated form of resistance and manipulation, and, therefore, it is a road that will bring is further away from home instead of closer.

Stopping your resistance: how do you do this in real life?

1. Enter the frightening or painful situation completely.

2. Allow it in, endure it and stop your resistance.

3. Notice and feel that you want to avoid and escape certain emotions and feelings.

4. Recognize that this is the core of every drama.

5. Don't try to shut out the feeling; instead, visualize a beautiful wooden door that you open wide with a big smile on your face.

6. Let everything that you're afraid of come in. Let it touch you.

7. Be full of trust and actually look forward to the next bad or uncomfortable feeling that comes your way and welcome it with open arms each and every time it knocks at your door.

8. You will start to notice that it will become far less frightening to simply feel things.

9. You will find that the wooden door will become your gateway to harmony and peace.

Summary

1} The search is a system that will always preserve and maintain itself. Over and over again, the searcher takes on a new 'truth' in the hope that this new truth will finally end his or her search.

2} The difficult thing about the endless search is that we still start from the ego's perspective: we want to improve ourselves and our life.

3} The ego gets absolutely no satisfaction in accepting the here and now; it's far too busy always looking ahead to the future, to the next moment and the moment after that. It says: 'Once, one day soon, when I have reached it, I will find peace and happiness.'

4} The further away the goal or target, the bigger the ego. So, by definition, spiritual people have a bigger ego. Their goal is not a new job or a bigger house; it goes well beyond that, even beyond all earthly things: salvation, enlightenment, God, immortality – that is their goal.

5} Spiritual people should therefore always remain cautious, extra vigilant and alert. Often what we do in the name of 'spirituality' is nothing more than a mutated form of resistance and manipulation, and therefore it is a road that will bring us further away from home instead of closer.

life is not
a fight that
needs to be won

A CONVERSATION WITH LYNNE MCTAGGART

*Life is a sea full of waves that we don't need to control,
but we can gain freedom by giving up
our resistance against it.*

– LYNNE MCTAGGART

I had an intriguing conversation with the amazing Lynne McTaggart about what spirituality is, including the abuse of spirituality, the power of intention, thoughts and acceptance. She is an award-winning investigative journalist and author of six books, among others *The Field*, *The Intention Experiment* and *The Bond – Connecting Through the Space Between Us*. You may also know her from the (sequel) scientific documentary *What the Bleep!? – Down the Rabbit Hole*. In the international newsletter *What Doctors Don't Tell You*, she brings to light the dangers of many medical treatments. She wants to empower the patient. She also publishes a monthly online magazine *Proof!*, in which thousands of alternative medicinal products are tested, rated and compared.

Lynne McTaggart is known for her groundbreaking research in the area of the zero point fields and how human consciousness relates to it. She has also shown us scientific proof of the power of intention. Lynne is one of the greatest authorities in this area; even Dan Brown became inspired by her in *The Lost Symbol*. Lynne's work is considered to be pioneering when it comes to creating a much-needed bridge between science and spirituality.

*

We need to regain our primal knowledge.

*

Lynne: "The mechanical world-view is past its due date and on its way out. We are on a bridge and moving towards a completely different outlook on science and on the world, because new science tells us that we are not separate from each other, animals, nature, the earth and the universe, but that everything is connected to everything, that separate worlds don't exist in reality, but that everything is, in fact, one. The ancient traditions already knew this. But now we have to return to this primal knowledge and understanding. As the American playwright and poet T. S. Eliot once said: 'We arrive where we started. And know the place for the first time.'"

The Bond
In her book *The Bond*, Lynne wrote about this kind of connection. When it comes to this type of knowledge, the kind

we need to return to and that we need to regain, the keyword for this connection is bond. She says: "If you see the world as a giant machine and humans as a survival mechanism, you can say that, technologically speaking, we have achieved a lot, but on a spiritual and metaphysical level these paradigms have led us to a most desperate and cruel kind of isolation and to a world full of rivalry, competition and survival of the fittest. The illusion of separation and the feeling that we end at the tip of the hairs on our skin means that we aren't interacting with the universe that we live in. This is, in fact, the biggest problem there is. Thankfully, science shows us that there is a different way and that we are far more than anyone has ever told us before. At the same time, we are far less individual than we ever suspected."

*

We are far more than anyone has ever told us.

*

"Frontier scientists in the field of biology, physics, psychology and sociology have each individually found evidence that there is a definite connection between the smallest particles in us, our bodies and surroundings, between ourselves and all people we are in contact with and between every member of all social groups. That connection is so deep and profound that it appears that there is no dividing line between one and the other. In essence, the world doesn't work based on the activity of individual things but by the connection, the 'space' between us.

"The most striking detail is perhaps," says Lynne, "that the latest data from all the different areas of science show us that man's natural drive isn't to be competitive, as was always assumed in the classic theory of evolution, but rather to find oneness and wholeness. All living beings, including man, come equipped with an instinctive urge for a continual search for a bond or connection, an urge that transcends all other urges, even the personal ones. They only grow and blossom when they feel part of a greater whole."

Survival of the fairest

"Still, the current view of the universe, for most people, is all about lack and scarcity and about you and I, us and nature, all the separated elements that have to fight each other in order to survive," I say. "Look at the economy, at how we interact with each other, with nature, animals and earth. I don't see a lot of people who live according to this, as you put it, primal, instinctive connection; from the realization that everything is connected; that in reality separate worlds don't exist, but that everything is, in fact, one; that we live in one big force field, where humanity and nature continually influence each other."

*

Man's natural drive isn't to be competitive,
but to find oneness and wholeness.

*

Lynne says: "Our current paradigm has its roots in traditional science; it is one of separation and, therefore, competition and survival. But we are now in a transition to a new time period. The crises we face in many areas – financial crises, a crisis of confidence – show us that the way we live now is not in accordance with our true nature as givers and sharers. And the fact that we are all slowly withdrawing indicates that we're going against our nature, that we think we have arrived at the end of something, and that all things will collapse. But what is actually collapsing is the wrong idea about who we really are. We have finally reached a point where we can no longer live according to our own limited and incorrect definitions of ourselves.

"Nature always moves in the direction of wholeness, and

we only live, grow and succeed when we follow that natural principle. So it is not a survival of the fittest. It is the survival of the fairest, survival of the most honest and the most genuine. What I mean by this is: we are meant to care, to share and be honest. That's how we work. Studies have shown us that we all come with an inherent it's-not-fair alert in our brain, and when things are very unfair, all of us suffer from it. Recent studies about all different types of societies show us that the countries that are considered most unfair – the ones that have the greatest inequality in incomes – also have the worst statistics in the field of all other social factors: healthcare, education, violence and crime. The USA is at the top of the list in these statistics. So when you really look at these statistics, it is clear that everyone – rich or poor – suffers when we are not honest."

*

We are meant to care, to share and be honest.

*

"Many of the scientific studies I looked into show us that it is in our nature to connect in every way possible – also to be selfless. Traditional science has always told us that we are essentially selfish, but this doesn't appear to be true. From a more recent scientific point of view, people are naturally healthy. And healthy people are natural givers and sharers. When we act against our nature and create a society that is not consistent with this, that's when the problems will arise."

The power of intention for the glory of the individual
But what about the hype around the power of intention? It suggests that an individual's life is sustainable; that it can be moulded and shaped into what you want and used for their own glory; that it can shape and create more material wealth; that it can influence your own physical health and personal life.

Lynne says: "When we think about ourselves, we think about ourselves as individuals because we think: 'My body and mind are unique. I am the master of my fate.' All these ideas convince us that we are all separate little islands who have to take care of ourselves separately and must arrange everything for ourselves alone. But nothing is further from the truth.

"An example. For a long time we believed that our genes predetermine everything about us and that they are unchangeable. From the latest scientific data – which we owe, among others, to the brilliant biologist Bruce Lipton – it appears that this concept is completely outdated. For instance, a test was done with mice that carried a gene for brain tumours. One mouse was isolated, the other wasn't. The outcome was that the isolated mouse developed far more tumours. The environment was the deciding factor in triggering the tumour gene.

"At the moment, there is an unbelievable amount of developments going on in science that show us that genes do not predetermine everything, that Darwin and neo-Darwinism were wrong and that the theory that a gene operates anatomically is just utter nonsense. A study about depression in Japan, for example, shows us that the Japanese tend to have a predisposition for depression. But on the other hand, the Japanese are much better at forming social groups than we are in the West. Because of that – and despite their predisposition for it – they suffer far less from depression than we do in the West. So this study also shows us that the main cause for depression is isolation. The whole theory of brain chemistry in relation to depression doesn't appear to be correct. Now we are beginning to see why, and we're starting to see depression and other illnesses as a part of a sociological phenomenon, determining whether or not we feel sheltered and safe, connected or disconnected."

*

*Use your energy to change your relationship with
the experience rather than changing the experience itself.*

*

"Our genes are activated (or not) by environmental influences: by your eating, life and thought patterns and emotions, by the air that you breathe, the water you drink, your relationships with others. In short: the total sum of how you live your life causes certain genes to be 'turned on' and activated or to be completely silenced. Furthermore, you could also say that we create our physical self from the outside in. So there is no such thing as a 'separated self'. Because: if everything outside of myself creates the person that I become, where does my 'I' begin and where does it end and where does the rest of the world begin? So I say: we create our bodies and create our lives from moment to moment by our ongoing relationship with everything outside of ourselves."

Living in combat

To create your own life and to consciously influence your health doesn't mean that you create a different reality with the power of intention and your thoughts, or change reality to what you want it to be. It means seeing that we have the ability to develop in relation to our experiences and our suffering, instead of being ruled by them. Pain and suffering are part of life, and we've developed all sorts of patterns to deal with them. Indeed, the vast majority these are cultivated. When we experience ennui and pain, we think we need to fight and we attack reality.

*

We are constantly busy trying to win the battle.

*

"Exactly," says Lynne. "That's just how we are programmed. But life is not a battle that needs to be won, and yet unconsciously we think otherwise. We fight against ourselves and others, against what takes place in reality – we fight in business and against ageing. We are constantly trying to win the battle. That kind of conditioning leads to stress and illness, like heart problems, instead of relaxation and good health. You can also ask yourself the question: 'OK, when there is pain or disappointment, let me see what is the best way to handle this.' Then you put your binoculars in a totally different position: you use your energy to change your relationship to the experience instead of changing the experience itself."

*

Creation is a 24-hour process
whether you are aware of it or not.

*

So, it's about acceptance and surrender? "Yes," Lynne says, "because that brings you a release and relaxation, and that relaxation has a major influence on your vibrational frequency with which you continuously create. The power of intention and thought are enormous. What many people do not realize is that you can have a beautiful higher thought during a moment in the day which is a conscious intention, but it is one that you constantly 'broadcast'. This means that the rest of the day you send out semi-unconscious thoughts and feelings that are based on, for example, old pain, anxiety, jealousy or greed. Creation is a 24-hour process, whether you are aware of it or not."

Unconscious sabotage

"*The Secret* completely bypassed the fact that you can also sabotage all your conscious intentions with your semi-unconscious intentions. Which, in turn, has everything to do with how you are programmed and how you programme yourself in life. You can meditate for half an hour a day and send out very direct positive intentions into the ether, but the rest of the day a completely different cassette tape is playing underneath the surface, one that says: you're doing this wrong, you're doing that wrong, you don't look good, you're not smart or witty enough, you're not worthy, you don't deserve it. As humans, we have an unbelievable amount of negative (often semi-unconscious) programmes and thoughts. And we also send those out into the universe. With all the consequences that they will entail. However, you can learn to shape or mould your negative thoughts. To become more conscious of your negative thoughts, you can, for example, learn to monitor your thoughts, to observe them. The next step is to replace those negative thoughts by positive thoughts. You will also have to tackle your unconscious, with often sabotaging convictions buried there. There are numerous helpful effective methods for this, like Eye Movement Desensitization and Reprocessing (EMDR) and Emotional Freedom Techniques (EFT)."

In agreement with reality

So does that mean we have control over everything? And: should we have that? Lynne: "I think that one of the biggest problems with the New Age Movement is that people begin to think that they have control over everything. But that obviously isn't the case. First of all, we're all connected and influence each other. So that also means that if, on an individual level, we all get what we want, it would create very big problems. Besides, some things just happen. If I walk outside right now and get hit by a bus, it's not my fault, unless I didn't look. We have to recognize that life sometimes has a different plan for us. It is a beautiful thing if you can trust in that."

*

There is an enormous power hidden
in being in agreement with reality.

*

I tell Lynne one of my favourite lines by Inti Cesar Melasquez: 'If there's something you need, it will come to you, on the condition that you are free. That is the cosmic law.' She says: "Exactly, that's what it's all about. To be free and unattached to whatever the outcome is. Edgar Mitchell, the astronaut, with whom I started The Field and Noetic Science (the science of the power of the human mind) when we began, always said: 'Just trust the process. Put out your empty cup and let the universe fill it.'

"To have faith and trust in the process, and not to be attached to a certain outcome, is a very important life lesson. I am old enough not to be afraid to say that there is an enormous power hidden in acceptance and surrender, in being in full agreement with reality. Often, you don't know why something happens because you are unable to see the gift that is hidden in it. But when I look back at my personal life, in hindsight every setback turned out to be a huge gift."

Self-help and other-help
"Most people try to become something instead of simply learning to be," says Lynne. "They have to go somewhere to find happiness: more money, power, status, fame, another partner, a different appearance. Most of us live in a paradigm of 'more, more, more' and 'better, better, better'. Spirituality is often abused in this way, often among the so-called spiritual masters. People who don't fundamentally transform or develop a deeper

consciousness are, in fact, abusing the term 'spirituality' and are still functioning from the ego. They are the same ego impulses. This is exactly the same game, only on a different platform."

*

*True spirituality is not only about the focus inward
but just as much about the outside.*

*

"The term 'spirituality' has sort of been taken hostage by the New Age movement. For many, it seems to be a type of workout schedule, like one you would follow at the gym. You go to the gym to work on your biceps. In New Age philosophy, you go inside to work on yourself. But no matter how noble and enlightened it may seem, it is usually a very selfish, ego-oriented activity." As for what she regards to be true spirituality, Lynne says: "We are here to learn, not just about how to get from A to B and how to be filled with constant joy and happiness. Life is not a standard recipe but one big rollercoaster. Life is a sea full of waves that we don't need to control, but we can gain freedom by giving up our resistance against it. That's living life beyond right or wrong; that's experiencing what is. A spiritual awakening means that you fully accept that reality.

"True spirituality is not only about the focus inward but just as much about the outside. To not only be involved with yourself, gazing in the mirror all day, but to also involve yourself with others. Spirituality is far less about self-help and much more about helping others. After all, the fundamental aspect of spirituality is altruism. This is learning to live in acceptance for the greater good of the whole. With this inner peace you can be a positive force in the world. Spirituality is the promoting of connection and oneness thinking. But it is about really living this. Spirituality is not something you only do on Sunday."

balance between 'doing' and 'being'

Enlightenment is understanding that there is nowhere to go,
nothing to do, and nobody you have to be except exactly
who you're being right now.

– NEALE DONALD WALSCH

Is acceptance the same as resignation?

Is acceptance the same as resignation? I hope that, as we near
the end of this book, you know that the answer to this question
is a resounding 'no'. This book isn't a proclamation to simply let
life waltz all over you, but rather an invitation to let go of our
iron-fist control.

I'd like to show you how we in our Western culture tend to classify everything as either good or bad. How we tend to think ahead or in the past and worry all the time. And how all of this is a continual form of duality in our thinking – and therefore our lives – that we've started to view as normal, but is, in fact, rather sickening.

Even if this is how we've been doing it for centuries in the West, it is not normal. When my Tibetan friend Tulka Lobsang visits the Netherlands, he always frowns when he observes the Dutch people. He looks with pure amazement at our tendency to always want to micromanage our happiness, and how doing so only brings us dissatisfaction and a sense of loss. It is very difficult for him to understand why it is so difficult for us to simply be, without a purpose, without guilt, without ifs or buts. He doesn't live in a world where you must 'work hard now so that in some distant future you can really live your life'.

Does happiness need a reason?

Is that laziness? No, it is something very different. It is living from the perspective that happiness doesn't need a reason. To him, there is no link between reaching a goal and experiencing happiness; it is a link only we Westerners seem to make. Just look at the coaching and training world. You must follow your heart and your passion, achieve your goals, make your dreams come true, know what your 'holy contract' here on earth is. If you don't, it will be impossible to find happiness.

*

*We have a real tendency to always want
to micromanage our happiness.*

*

But what if you don't find your life goal? Does that mean you cannot be happy? What if what you do for a living doesn't express your passion and ideals? Would that forfeit your right or possibility for happiness? Oh, please! How many times in my life did I pursue a goal and, once I had achieved it, did I find myself surprised at the fact that I still didn't feel that inner peace? I discovered something because of that: namely, that the direct link that we think there is between achieving your goal, or realizing a dream, and finding or experiencing happiness is a lie. That would be the same thing as thinking that happiness and inner peace are only found somewhere beyond the reality of this very moment.

It means that we believe that our happiness is dependent on something outside of ourselves; that there is an external magic salvation or solution outside of ourselves; a different lifestyle, a different job, a new husband or wife, a different car, a long journey, a house at the beach or a great accomplishment. And who says that once you connect with your life's mission that everything automatically falls into place and suddenly everything becomes easy? That you have somehow tapped into some permanent source of happiness? Well, I can tell you from experience: I am – for as far as I feel and know – connected to my life's mission, but that doesn't mean I don't have to make sure I constantly stay aware and alert, pay attention to my resistance, and, over and over again, have to offer more space for reality and make choices that facilitate more ease and relaxation in the moment.

*

*You don't feel better because you achieved your goal,
but because temporarily you don't have to strive or do.*

*

Isn't achieving a goal or realizing a dream fulfilling? Doesn't it give you a good feeling? Sure it does! But only for a brief moment. And not so much because you achieved your goal, but because you can finally stop striving and doing. You earned your moment of freedom, you can relax without guilt and finally surrender to the shapeless world of the now.

It is not the achieved goal that does this. No, it's the fact that you are temporarily relieved from your striving pattern. That is the really good feeling you have when you achieve your goal. Until ... the searching and striving urge returns. Then there are new dreams to dream and new goals to achieve. For so many people, this is a lifelong and never-ending marathon, and they never realize why all those goals don't seem to bring them happiness and why they constantly need new ones. To find real peace in your life, it is important to see this clearly.

*

My life became far more interesting
the moment I stopped thinking that it
should be more interesting.

*

However, I know a lot of people who worry daily because they feel they aren't connected to their life's mission, who have no idea why they are here or what their destination is. So when I say to them: do you want to know what your destination is? Well, take a look around you. It is this very moment and the way your life is right now. This is it. It is just as it should be. You can find all the causes, solutions and answers right now. Usually the answer is, "Is it really that easy?" Oh yes, it really is that easy!

When someone says to me, "I'm so unhappy because I don't know what to do with my life and because I don't do anything 'special'", the only logical response is: "Relax into that reality, surrender yourself to your frustration, to the fact that you don't know right now, and allow your consciousness to realize that you may never know!" Believe me, I used to be a hardcore rationalizer, but have since experienced so many times that the moment I stopped trying to find the answers and solutions through my thinking, the answers came on their own. At a certain point I found myself doing things that gave me inner peace and satisfaction and which were a true expression of who I really was. That was because I took my thinking out of the equation – my 'I' wasn't around to create static or noise. My life became far more interesting, exciting and meaningful the moment I stopped thinking that it should be more interesting and meaningful.

Exercise: Close down the administration office in your head
Do you feel a lot of turmoil, frustration, a sense of emptiness – a void in your life – or do you have the feeling you keep missing the boat? Then I have a really fun exercise for you: close down the administration office in your head and send your 'I' on a holiday to Bora Bora. Picture yourself putting the CLOSED sign in the window. The 'thinking' and 'I' are on holiday. And that's a very good thing. Because these two only cause us endless worry and concern.

Being present is your birthright
If we believe we cannot be happy right now, then it's time to look at our conditioning. It's all the little stories our brain has thought up so it can keep postponing our happiness. We have all been conditioned to believe we cannot be happy until we know our life's purpose. It is our Christian, Calvinistic way of thinking that has caused us to think that happiness is something you have to earn, and that inner peace is something you have to work hard for.

*

Happiness is not about 'doing', but about 'being'.

*

My dear Tibetan friend Tulku Lobsang does his teachings and afterwards eats his meal with his full attention and then relaxes. He lives in a far greater sense of surrender, and it's far easier for him to switch between doing and being. The 'do' mode is a tool he uses to do what's necessary, but as soon as he is done, he turns off the switch. Happiness is not about 'doing', but about 'being'. Something we can barely comprehend or understand here in the West, with our internal and external 'to do' lists.

Tulku isn't preoccupied with the fight or the struggle. If someone tries to attack him, his answer always begins with a bright and generous smile invariably followed by the meaningless words 'Yes, yes. Please, please.' A great comeback, as he always remains neutral. I find myself using these words more and more (in my mind, because I find that that is enough). When someone in the audience once asked Tulku why he was seated on a higher table when he always emphasizes and speaks about reducing the ego, his answer was: "I'm sitting here to reduce your ego!" followed by a roaring laugh. He doesn't think 'What a stupid question', doesn't judge and doesn't apply dividing lines to reality. By doing this, he can simply be.

*

Paradoxically, people with chronic pain can only win the battle against the pain by giving up the fight.

*

There is something very real we as Westerners can learn from Tulku. That is: you can choose your attitude towards your experience. You can develop how you relate to pain and disappointment instead of being ruled by them. We Westerners tend to jump to conclusions and instantly determine our position at even the slightest provocation. 'Pain? Oh help, I have to do something about that right away!' What if we would try and practise a little more neutrality, shifting our attitude towards 'OK, I feel pain, let's see if I can allow this pain in, without judgement and without feeling that I have do something about it.' Again, you use your energy to change your attitude towards the experience instead of trying to change the experience itself. That way, we depart from the land of duality and enter into a world of oneness and wholeness; we create a life without dividing lines between happiness or misfortune, being unhappy or happy, one or the other.

Acceptance & Commitment Therapy
I read an interesting article in the Dutch journal *Revalidatie Magazine*. The article was about the so-called Acceptance & Commitment therapy used in pain management in the Netherlands. It asserted, paradoxically, that people with chronic pain can only win the battle against pain by giving up the fight against it. Someone asks for help because they want to get rid of the pain, but this therapy is actually aimed at learning to live with the pain. So, in order for the therapy to succeed, the patient has to let go of their most important motivation for pain treatment. The concept of this method is that much of our suffering is caused by our attempts to avoid the pain. Those who have experienced chronic pain, something I know all too well, cannot avoid the pain. As a matter of fact, chronic pain problems will often continue and get worse by constantly trying to fight or control the pain. Therefore, this therapy aims at having the patient continuing to do the things they love to do, while, at the same time, consciously accepting the pain, negative thoughts and experiences.

*

Use your energy to change your attitude towards the experience instead of trying to change the experience itself.

*

And so we return to the core of what acceptance is all about: to eliminate our dualistic thinking. If you think dualistically, then the pain is not allowed to be there and must be fought off; it doesn't matter how many pills or powders it takes. If that doesn't work, you have two choices: to continue to fight or to get stuck in your victim role. Both will lead to total stagnation and will block the natural, vital flow of life. They don't lead to improvement or progress but to a complete standstill, decay and decline.

We should all actually apply the Acceptance & Commitment Therapy to our daily lives. It offers a far more realistic view on life than thinking 'pain is bad' and, instead of going into resistance mode with everything that happens, moving along with the natural rhythm of our lives. That leads to a life beyond wrong and right, to being fully present and fully experiencing what is.

Summary

1} Is acceptance the same as resignation? I hope that, as we near the end of this book, you know that the answer to this question is 'no'. This book isn't a proclamation to just let life waltz all over you, but rather an invitation to let go of our iron-fist control.

2} Acceptance is living in the realization that happiness doesn't need a reason. That in reality there is no direct link between reaching a goal and experiencing happiness: a link only we Westerners seem to make. That would be the same as thinking that happiness and inner peace are only found somewhere beyond the reality of this very moment.

3} If we believe we cannot be happy right now, then it's time to look at our conditioning. It's all the little stories our brain has thought up so it can keep postponing our happiness.

4} We have all been conditioned to believe that we cannot be happy until we know life's purpose. It is our Christian, Calvinistic thinking that has caused us to think that happiness is something you have to earn and that inner peace is something you have to work hard for. Happiness is not about 'doing' but about 'being'.

constructing your inner infrastructure

A CONVERSATION WITH PROFESSOR WILLIAM TILLER

The point is that we express ourselves as we really are.

It's important to start expressing ourselves as we really are. I had a fascinating conversation with Dr William Tiller about acceptance. William Tiller is a professor emeritus at Stanford University and a co-founder of the Institute of Noetic Sciences and the Academy of Parapsychology and Medicine. Throughout most of his career, he has been a professor at the Department of Materials Science and Engineering at the University of Stanford, and his areas of expertise include metallurgy, crystallization and semiconductor materials.

In the sixties, he began a whole new career in a field that had always interested him: the study of the paranormal and unexplained areas of the human consciousness. His research was aimed at creating a bridge between modern science and spirituality. This is why he applied very strict scientific protocols in his research so that he could attract serious attention from other scientists.

*

His research was aimed at bridging the gap between modern science and spirituality.

*

He became interested in the study of subtle energies such as Reiki energy and developed a kind of ultra-sensitive Geiger counter to measure the subtle energies emitted from the hands of the Reiki practitioner. In doing so, he showed the existence of an energy field that is not in the electromagnetic spectrum.

During his research, Professor Tiller noticed that the healing intention that was sent to the hands of the Reike practitioner had a crucial effect on the measured energy. After finishing these experiments, he concluded that the human intention by way of our thoughts and feelings has a measurable effect on our physical reality. He also tested qigong masters and discovered that their hands had a healing magnetism with a strength similar to a magnetic strength of 20,000 gauss. Their palms radiated a type of infrared light (from 1 to 4.5 microns in wavelength) that proved to possess real healing properties.

Pioneering experiments
Tiller conducted a series of experiments to study the possible effect of human intention, in which he only made use of strictly scientific protocols. He then built a machine that he named the Intention Imprinted Electrical Device, abbreviated as IIED, which

radiated a weak electromagnetic energy with the capacity of less than one millionth of a watt. He asked four well-trained people to enter a deep state of meditation and to imprint their intention of the upcoming experiment into the IIED. Subsequently, the experiment was carried out with two identical IIEDs, of which one was imprinted through the meditative process, while the other machine was left alone. The imprinted IIEDs were displayed in separate rooms for the participants. And what happened? The acidity (pH) level of water could be intentionally increased or decreased, the activity of the human liver enzyme could be increased 15 to 30 per cent, and the growth rate of a fruit fly larvae could be accelerated by 25 per cent.

*

Nothing just comes falling from the sky,
no matter how hard you visualize, wish or want it.

*

With these experiments, Tiller proved that the power of human intention has a measurable effect on our physical reality. And after three or four months of testing, he discovered that the effects of the experiments continued, even after the IIEDs were removed from the spaces. Somehow even the test rooms were influenced. The measuring device was no longer needed to achieve the same effect.

Pioneer
Professor Tiller is a true pioneer and considered by many to be the 'new Einstein of science'. When I speak to him about creation and manifestation, the power of intention and thoughts and the effect they have on our lives, he immediately brings up the subject of our personal responsibility. He says: "Nothing just comes falling from the sky, no matter how hard you visualize, wish or want it. What is important is that you build your own

inner infrastructure so you can become who you want to be and so you can get what you want."

*

Your emotions, thoughts and feelings move a billion times faster than the speed of light.

*

"By that I mean: you first have to ready and prepare yourself on the inside. In quantum terms: you first need to build yourself up 'informatively' from the inside. You build up this inner infrastructure with the experiences in your life. The more infrastructure you build up, the more spirit enters your system, the more conscious you become.

"A lot of information moves a billion times faster than the speed of light. So it is not directly accessible for us. The reason we can't see it is because it has a very high vibrational frequency. There are energetic layers all around us that work in interaction with the cosmos. This is what is so extraordinary about our earthly existence: the largest part of our reality is on the inside – neither visible nor measurable, but the deciding factor for everything there is, as your inner core is your magnet. Your emotions, thoughts and feelings move a billion times faster than the speed of light. Therefore, you may not be able to see them, but they have an absolute effect on everything around you."

The physical vacuum
"We have to build up an inner infrastructure so that we can become conscious on many different levels. We can do that by seriously entering into silence and to learn to listen to what takes place in the physical vacuum. That way, we can become conscious of the greater whole of which we are all a part of, and feel at one with the source and come into contact with the higher dimensional information.

"It's important that you do your inner homework; it's just like going to the gym to pump up your outward appearance. Only you're doing it on the inside. You can do this in many ways: yoga, qigong, heartmath or Sufism. We are co-creators, and so, in essence, we are also responsible for all the problems in the world. We are not outside of the creation process, but we are a real part of it. If you don't like the things taking place outside of yourself, then it is important to realize that you were a co-creator of them.

"The more inner infrastructure we build up, the more we become conscious of our power and strength, and that we can make use of the immeasurable energy that is available to us, cosmically speaking. We are still at the early stages of this process. Of course, above all, we are souls having a physical experience. Our spiritual ancestors have entrusted us with these physical bodies and placed us in this playpen we call the universe so we can grow up in coherency and, together with them, become co-creators."

*

Currently you can see a clear division:
people who move in the direction of the light
and those who do not.

*

"Let me tell you something about coherency. Do you see this lamp? I estimate it's about 45 watts. It gives us light, but not a lot of light because it is mostly incoherent. This means there is a lot of destructive disturbance to the light waves. This also means that if you use your consciousness in a way so that every light wave connects to the previous one and the following one, the energy density of the light particles would become ten times the light that comes from the surface of the sun."

Radiate what you are

"I can see you thinking: how do I apply what you're explaining to my personal life?" William Tiller laughs. "By going inward, to learn how to get into contact with the silence and your deepest being. That way, you become part of the creation process, come into contact with the Source, and you put certain things in motion. The soul connects to the Source through our experiences. The more experience you gain, the more you, informatively speaking, build up the inner infrastructure in yourself, and the more you radiate what you are. We are so much more than what has been manifested so far and what we manifest in each moment. But that's OK. This is only one period in the history of Earth and humanity."

*

It is important we start to express ourselves as we really are.

*

"At the moment you can see a clear division: people who move in the direction of the light and those who do not. And that division will only become bigger. We are the product of the process. And everything in this classroom of our earthly life has been arranged and thought up just as it should be so we can grow. There is no coincidence in that."

'What about our free will,' I ask Tiller. He says: "Free will does exist to a certain extent. When you take away free will from a human, it becomes impossible for them to grow. The choice is necessary. If you don't see the pitfalls in life, you have to continue to plough through the mess until you become conscious of the pitfalls. You decide. That free will is your only teacher. Everything that you can imagine can become reality; all choices and all possibilities and circumstances. But everything comes down to making the choice to eventually become that coherent light source that you essentially already are. This is why we have to develop ourselves, to become more conscious and to take part in this life."

Free will

"We become more conscious by becoming the answer to the experiences ourselves in this earthly classroom. How you react to those experiences shows where you are in the process of consciousness, in building up your inner infrastructure. The goal of this whole process is not to become who you really are. No, the goal is to start expressing yourself more as you really are.

"The soul is like a storage space of the wisdom gained from our experiences during many, many, many lives. And the soul has to go through all possible stages of experience to gain more knowledge. Each moment again we have the choice: are we consciously moving up or down? It can also be that a person comes to a standstill or stops developing. This is why 're-embodiment' or 'rebirth' is so important. That way, you can return to a new body, with a whole new family and different life experiences. You imprint many of these before you even enter your new life – something you remember nothing about, of course."

The ego blocks surrender

"The point is that you develop throughout all these lives and begin to see the world with your heart instead of your head. Your brain, your thoughts and your ego are helpful and important in life, but eventually you will come to realize that when you help someone else build themselves up from the inside, you also build yourself up. Just look at you, Annemarie; this is why you write books and do the things you do.

"To discover this is a very long process, because the ego is in the way. The way I see it, there are three stages in the development of the human consciousness. The first part is the 'rising stage', which we all go through in the area of our upbringing, education, relationships, sports and work. All those experiences help us build our inner infrastructure. The second stage is the 'surrender stage', which is by far the most difficult stage because the ego wants to protect itself and wants to hold on tight to its own familiar, old ideas in order to maintain the delusion of safety. This protection of the ego stands in the way of the acceptance and surrender. Because when you surrender, it means that you also have trust; trust that the universe has the best intentions with you. The third stage is the 'descending stage', and that's when the universe works through you."

*

In order for the intention experiment to succeed,
you must let go of any and all attachments to the outcome.

*

"So in the end, surrender is essential in achieving the ultimate way of working together with the universe. Surrender is difficult to learn. The only way to surrender is by travelling inward and to connect to the silence in yourself. By meditating on the body and continuing to go beyond the body. That is how you connect to everything that is essential, infinite and indestructible; to the greater universe which is always stable and unshakable; to everything that we are in essence."

Surrender and creation: Two in one

This type of surrender is crucial in any creation process, as Tiller goes on to explain: "There is a big difference between the power of intention and thoughts and the power of acceptance and surrender. With the experiments we work carefully and with great detail. I write very specific intention statements for each experiment, and when we do an experiment it is always with people who have a lot of meditation experience. We enter the silence, connect to the unseen and express the particular intention. We hold that intention for about 15 minutes and always repeat the experiment once, maybe twice. But we never repeat an experiment a third time. Why not? Because then we are no longer creating, but we are manipulating. After every session we end the experiment by saying in our mind: 'Thy will shall be done.' In order for the intention experiment to succeed, you must let go of any and all attachments to the outcome.

"If we used the combination of the power of intention and acceptance on a larger scale, we could have a deep and all-encompassing influence on the world. For example, you could use it to change global warming. But sadly, the weakest link in the whole is man. When people don't properly build themselves up from the inside, don't build that inner infrastructure, we cannot be good 'pumper-uppers', but instead we are 'pumper-downers', and the process doesn't work.

"We haven't learned how to use the power of intention for the greater good, and that's why it doesn't work. We only use the power of intention for ourselves, and even that we don't do right. Obviously, *The Secret* was too simplistic and put many people on the wrong track. People really believed this was the answer to all their problems and that they had to do very little for it. The great success of the *The Secret* made it clear to me where the world is in its development."

The lessons of Atlantis
"We are in a transition period to a new era – this is clear. Everything happening in the world is a symptom of this. This transition will take time, but in the new era we will have access to the higher energies I spoke of before. However, I believe, contrary to many others, that it will take a few centuries before we get there. But time is always difficult to predict.

"The world isn't going to end, but at the moment we find ourselves in the turbulent parts of the river of life, which may very well lead to a waterfall. It is a process we must go through. This has obviously happened before. First, there was the MU era, followed by the Lemure era and then the golden age of Atlantis. In the Atlantis era, there was clearly an abuse of knowledge, power, strength and energy, and you can see all of that happening again today. We live in a corrupt and greedy world in which power systems rule and turn people into slaves, nobody is satisfied with what they have, and everyone is constantly striving for better and more. Just look at the economy, the financial system and the divisions in our world. None of it makes any sense. If we as a race cannot get this together, why would the unseen powers want to continue to help us? We would only infect the universe with negativity and destructiveness."

*

Being is rooted in surrender.

*

"We live in a time of now or never. We have the ability to create a real change in consciousness and, in doing so, to greatly improve the world. But the hard work that is necessary is not being done by us at the moment but by the unseen powers and forces. And they will continue to support us if we show we are ready to take our responsibility and want to cooperate. Those are the rules of the game. That is why it is so important that people work on their inner infrastructure, because then you're even radiating healing when doing the dishes. It is about who you are and what you give to others in the best possible way in this moment. That is healing. Healing means you are deeply rooted. And being is deeply rooted in surrender. You cannot be fully present without surrender because surrender is your connection to the universe.

"How things will end for humanity? I am not sure. I'm just riding the river, with a calm curiosity for what will come my way."

in closing

Stepping out of reactivity

Living in acceptance is living in freedom. It has nothing to do with laziness, passiveness or patience, but actually leads to a proactive, participating and dynamic life. The only thing we truly have is this moment and the possibility of seeing how we can relate to the reality of this very moment: are we offering resistance against what is or do we surrender to it?

*

Does acceptance mean we should simply agree with everything?

*

It is about consciously dealing with the challenges that come your way and taking a good look at your natural tendencies and your conditional patterns. That way, you step out of reactivity; the circle of unconsciously getting stuck in your reactions and continuing to do so. All the things that make you say 'So now what do I do?' or 'How is this going to work out?' or 'What am I supposed to do with this?' are all practice material to help you get to a higher grade of acceptance. There is no better place to practise this than in your everyday life. No expensive acceptance coaching or another seminar or guru. No, your training ground is supplied to you every single day – free of charge – by life itself. Each moment is an amazing chance to not change the situation itself, but how you relate to it.

Acceptance or non-acceptance?

So, does acceptance mean we should simply agree with everything, think everything is just fine and with every challenge say, 'That's life?' No, not at all. If there is one thing I don't want to do with this book, it is to create 'spiritual softies' everywhere. I tend to have an allergic reaction and all my alarm bells go off when I see people who frantically try to appear all perfect and holy, people you can never challenge or who cannot be assertive. People like that don't exist and they don't need to. There is no contradiction between acting in an assertive manner and living in acceptance. In fact, the opposite is true. Let me give you a personal example. When someone continually undermines me, underestimates me and wants to put me down, I say to that person, 'This doesn't feel like a real conversation to me. Can you stop with this or we may as well end this conversation right now.' Or I just leave. Of course, it would be ridiculous to think, 'I live in acceptance so I will just let that person walk all over me.'

*

In order to get something,
you should actually no longer want it.
That is a cosmic law.

*

This doesn't mean that I don't accept the situation as it is, but that I simply respond to it from a place of self-worth and according to what the situation asks of me. Living in acceptance in no way means that you should just let people walk all over you if you don't want them to. I do, however, want to stay neutral in my reaction; I notice something that I don't find pleasant and say something about it, but I try to take my judgement about the situation, myself and others out of the equation, something I obviously don't always succeed in. But what is important is that your own thoughts don't take over, and that you don't attach any complicated stories, judgements, assumptions and conclusions to it, like 'What a jerk.' Or: 'Why would someone do this to me? I accept that there are people who do this. But don't do it to me and not in my house! Period.'

Not living in acceptance would mean having all these thoughts and opinions and being completely irritated on the inside, but then not saying or doing anything because I was afraid that someone will have an opinion about me. This is pure avoidance and a behaviour that comes from a fear of consequences, which, therefore, leads to impurity. I cannot determine for you when you should or should not act assertively. Sometimes I think to myself, 'What I hear is a load of rubbish, but I'm going to let it pass, I'm OK with that.' That's OK, too. It's about finding the balance that works for you in this; that you understand the mental resistance in your mind. Not taking action is not acceptance but actually non-acceptance.

*

*There's a powerful pulling force hidden inside
our inner independence and freedom.*

*

I hope that, with this book, I have shown you that the personal sustainability of our existence is mostly found in accepting participation, not in manipulating reality because we don't like what it has to offer us at the moment. I once received an email from someone who wrote angrily: 'Dear Annemarie, what is it with you and all that acceptance and surrender business? Haven't you heard that we can influence our own lives, that we can shape our own existence?'

Well, yes, I have heard that, and I think my own life is a perfect example of this. But it becomes dangerous when we think we are omnipotent; when we – from our thinking and doing mode – feel we can mould and shape our lives into precisely what we want, as long as we really apply ourselves and do our very best. We think we have more control than we do. It is a real Western disease to hold our own thoughts in such high regard. We identify ourselves with it and begin to see it as truth and reality.

Not fighting but studying

So if you find yourself still unhappy after all that mental pushing and shoving, then it's your own fault and twice as painful. That's why, from my personal experience, I am convinced we only receive the things in life that do not come from a place of neediness. So, in order to get something, you actually have to stop wanting it. That is a cosmic law. There's a powerful pulling force hidden inside our inner independence and freedom. Letting go of the reins on our will has a great effect on the quality of our lives. All that planning and arranging seems to be a necessity in our everyday lives, but if we do this with a little more ease, that is, with the realization that nothing is really under our control anyway, we will find it much easier to deal with surprises and changes. Did it go as we hoped or wished? Great! No? That's fine, too.

*

Live a life that is truly yours.
The total experience.
That's what it's all about!

*

Life is full of secrets, and in that labyrinth of mysteries we only know one thing for certain: there will always be changes and unexpected events taking place in our life. The true healing power of acceptance is to reconcile ourselves with that fact and to find our inner freedom within that uncertainty.

If, after you finish reading this book, you find yourself taking a breather in the sun or have the opportunity to enjoy a beautiful sunset, see if you can do this: be fully present. Do you feel the sun? Do you really see the sunset? Study everything that happens around you with a big smile on your face. Don't think, 'I have to enjoy this now.' No, try it even when you don't succeed – because you're thinking about all the things you still have to do to get there – just be and stay away from any and all judgements. Buddha taught us: don't fight, but study. Be kind to your experiences of this moment. Live a life that is truly yours. The total experience. That's what it's all about!

special thanks

Father Titus Brandsma for the inspiration he gives me.

Liesbeth Bakker, Bliz Events (www.blizevents.com)

Dr Eric Pearl (www.thereconnection.com)

Lynne McTaggart (www.lynnemctaggart.com)

Konstantin Korotkov (www.korotkov.org)

Dr Joe Dispenza (www.drjoedispenza.com)

Gregg Braden (www.greggbraden.com)

Prof William A Tiller (www.tillerfoundation.com)

And to the makers of www.thelivingmatrix.com

bibliography

Dreamer, Oriah Mountain, *Reis naar het binnenste van de Ziel*, House of Books, Vianen, 2001

Pearl, Eric, *De reconnectie*, Petiet, Barchem, 2006

Pierrakos, Eva, *Werken aan jezelf of juist niet?*, Ankh-Hermes, Deventer, 1995

Postma, Annemarie, *Het leven is perfect*, Forum, Amsterdam, 2008

Postma, Annemarie, *Liefde maken*, Forum, Amsterdam, 2007

Postma, Annemarie, *The Deeper Secret*, Watkins, London, 2012

Revalidatie Magazine (RM), year 16, number 4, December, 2010

Schipper, Kristofer, *Zhuang Zi*, August, Amsterdam, 2011

Thich Nhat Hanh, *Omarm je woede*, Asoka, Rotterdam, 2009

Zens Magazine for Meaning and Spirituality, number 7/8, article Karin de Mik, Hilversum, 2007

Zens Magazine for Meaning and Spirituality, number 7/8, interview with Annemiek Schrijver, Hilversum, 2007

Translation by Jordan Sowle at Sowle 2 Soul Translations (www.Sowle2Soul.com)